Kids Play

D0730959

Kids Play

Igniting Children's Creativity

Michele Cassou

JEREMY P. TARCHER / PENGUIN
A MEMBER OF PENGUIN GROUP (USA) INC.
NEW YORK

Most Tarcher/Penguin books are available at special quantity discounts for bulk purchase for sales promotions, premiums, fund-raising, and educational needs. Special books or book excerpts also can be created to fit specific needs. For details, write Penguin Group (USA) Inc. Special Markets, 375 Hudson Street, New York, NY 10014.

Jeremy P. Tarcher/Penguin
a member of
Penguin Group (USA) Inc.
375 Hudson Street
New York, NY 10014
www.penguin.com

Library of Congress Cataloging-in-Publication Data

Cassou, Michele.
Kids play : igniting children's creativity / by Michele Cassou.
p.   cm.
ISBN 1-58542-328-9
1. Painting—Study and teaching (Elementary)—United States.
2. Creative ability in children.   I. Title.
N362.C295   2004
372.5'2044'0973—dc22   2004046022

Printed in the United States of America
1   3   5   7   9   10   8   6   4   2

This book is printed on acid-free paper. ∞

ILLUSTRATIONS BY MICHELE CASSOU

BOOK DESIGN BY DEBORAH KERNER/DANCING BEARS DESIGN

To my granddaughters
Nina and Lea
with love

Contents

CHAPTER THREE

Creativity as Adventure and Exploration *85*

CHAPTER FOUR

Keeping Freedom and the Creative Spirit Alive *117*

CHAPTER FIVE

Deepening Understanding of the Creative Process   *153*

Appendix: Art Supplies and Where to Buy Them   *183*

This Book . . .

I wrote *Kids Play* out of love for children and their creative energy. Painting with children has helped me enter the depth of my creative passion, and I want to give back to them the treasures I uncovered.

This book reveals the essence of creativity as *play* and *self-expression*. It also shows the *dramatically important role* parents and teachers can play as guides and catalysts and how they can help remove obstacles to *jump-start* their children's creative power. *Kids Play* presents the Point Zero method for children's creativity, which is designed to introduce children to the wonderful activity of *painting as a process of exploration*. This unique method safeguards children's natural creativity and aims to fulfill its potential. In this book parents and teachers will also find ways to reestablish a direct connection between children and their creative power when it is lost and restore their enthusiasm to create.

When stimulated creativity reaches every aspect of children's lives, developing their inner potential and *self-confidence* while they grow, enhanced *self-esteem* and *self-reliance* are direct by-products. Through this method children learn to inhabit their feelings, to authentically manifest who they are, and to explore their world. The basic principles developed in this book are:

- Creativity as *play, adventure, and self-expression*
- Creativity as *process not product*
- Using *intuition and spontaneity* as the fuel and fire of creation
- Creativity as a tool to enhance children's lives

Written for parents and teachers, *Kids Play* explains how the creative process works, explores the most conducive contexts for creativity, and also suggests:

- What parents and teachers can do during the stages of creation
- What to avoid in safeguarding children's creative inspiration
- How guiding children can be a unique opportunity for adults to rediscover their own creativity

This book shows how precious creativity is for children and shows how to give them real support and appropriate guidance based on clarity of understanding and practical communication.

If you want your children to create from their hearts and souls, and if you want to know what they really need to become lastingly creative, read their stories throughout this book. A larger understanding and respect for your children's creativity will make you the guardian of their sacred space of creation.

Kids Play

CHAPTER ONE

A Magical Context
for the Creative Process

This chapter aims to inspire parents and teachers to create a context of *understanding and safety* for children's creativity by:

- **E**xploring the role of creativity in children's lives
- **L**ooking at the main obstacles to creativity
- **G**etting acquainted with the Point Zero method
- **C**reating a magical and safe place in which children can paint
- **L**ooking at their roles and responsibilities in the development of the creative process
- **D**ealing with their own *issues* of creativity

How I Started Working with Children

May what I do flow from me like a river

no forcing, no holding back

the way it is with children.

—RAINER MARIA RILKE

Discovering my creative passion in my early twenties was a turning point in my life. I was thrilled to have found such a powerful connection between creativity and self-expression. I felt immediately drawn to tell others about my experience and to inspire them to explore painting. I believed that freedom from product was the key element of the creative force, and I thought it was enough to start teaching. With great excitement I welcomed a small group of children into a makeshift studio in my home and unknowingly started my lifelong teaching career.

To my dismay I soon found that my enthusiasm was not always enough to inspire the depth of expression and the joy to create in children. Working with them was especially challenging because they easily became restless, bored, or self-critical. I was puzzled that children wouldn't grab at such a wonderful opportunity to be free and express themselves. It became obvious that I had work to do. I needed to explore teaching by questioning my basic assumptions about the creative process. I listened carefully to children, to their words and mostly in between them; I observed with

Only one apple for the whole class!

great attention their painting habits, their needs and longings. I also observed alertly the mystery of my own painting process.

On my way to becoming a teacher I made many mistakes. Some of my teachings, based on incomplete understanding, would backfire, for instance when I would try to push children toward freedom as a requirement instead of inspiring them to be free, or when I attempted to make children finish their paintings in a somewhat forceful way, as if it were a rule. Each time I watched my interaction take away a piece of their freedom and confidence it would break my heart and bring urgency to develop my teachings.

I came to realize how the *intelligence* of creativity works and how everything in it has to come from the child. Creativity needed to be offered as play, adventure, and self-expression. Putting pressures or expectations on children had to be banned; at the same time, the basic principles of creativity could never be compromised. Consequently, the creative process couldn't be taught as a technique because it is a *living process*. I needed to use my intuition and my heart, not my ideas of what was right. I had to become supple, available, and strong in the understanding of my own creativity. Within a few years I developed a method based on *process,* not techniques.

This method looks at the movement of creativity in a larger context, including the heart and the soul, and for the long-term benefit of children. This approach resulted in children entering true *process,* finding self-expression, and developing a solid base for creativity in their lives, an experience they couldn't forget.

The first time I was able to guide a little girl to her creative passion I saw the tender way she looked at me, and my joy knew no bounds. She looked at me as if I were a precious friend. Within a few weeks other children followed her creative steps, one by one letting go of fears and worries. In their eyes the traditional teacher disappeared; I had become someone they could count on for support and guidance, and I delighted in that role.

This teaching is a gentle process that follows children's journeys *into themselves.* When children reach their inner being and express themselves, their hearts open. When they are not only accepted but also appreciated for who they are, they give back.

Soon the children relied on me to understand them and be with them during good and bad times. The first sign of their trust would often come when they by "mistake" called me "Mamma" or "Dad" or even the name of someone else they felt close to. Sometimes they caught themselves mixing our names and smiled, hands on their mouths, but often they were totally unaware of doing so. Fear had left them, the studio had become a truly safe place, and their creativity could now flower.

Creativity Belongs to Children

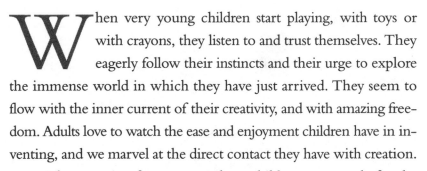

*The most beautiful thing we can
experience is the mysterious. It is the
source of all true art and science.*

—ALBERT EINSTEIN

When very young children start playing, with toys or
with crayons, they listen to and trust themselves. They
eagerly follow their instincts and their urge to explore
the immense world in which they have just arrived. They seem to
flow with the inner current of their creativity, and with amazing freedom. Adults love to watch the ease and enjoyment children have in inventing, and we marvel at the direct contact they have with creation.

When coming from a pure place, children create only for the
sake of play and for the thrill of inventing, never for a projected
result. They create from the center of their being, an authentic
place, unpolluted, unconditioned, a place that does not suffer any
influences or any limitations of form or content. I call that place
Point Zero; in it, *the doing is all that matters.* Point Zero, the source
of creation, holds immense potential in all children; it is fully alive
and present from the beginning.

Born from Point Zero, the creative force offers a marvelous tool
for children to fulfill their need to express themselves, to grow and to
explore their world. Soon, however, through classes or criticisms, the

notion of good and bad product is introduced into children's lives. That notion generates a separation and a struggle between them and their creative play. When this middle step is interposed with its expectations, *children are pressured into following rules and blueprints instead of their intuition*. The true source of creation is abandoned and creative passion is lost. The connection with Point Zero is broken, and creativity becomes a mental activity; the children start to struggle for inspiration, and the pressure for achievement starts.

Creativity does not dwell just in the mystery; it is also very practical. When children learn to listen to themselves through creativity, they also learn to think for themselves and trust their feelings. Intuition is a wise, strong, and authentic voice that guides children to trust and express themselves. *Intuition is the moving force of creativity*; it is the fuel that maintains inspiration and brings about self-expression. Through the use of intuition, children become self-reliant; self-esteem and self-confidence develop, which enhance the way they respond to the world.

Children must discover that what they need to create is *already inside them*: an unlimited potential of play and inspiration. They must discover that they do not need to be taught everything and that creativity is a place without limits. The belief that they need models and instruction to create makes them dependent and uncertain about who they are and what they feel.

This is when parents, teachers, and other adults have a role to play. They can help preserve that endless source of passion in which children can explore anything about their world and their dreams without fear.

It is a great gift to children to show them how to use and respect their spontaneous intuition and to have them discover the magical surprises of creativity: a creativity that comes from a pure intimate source, from Point Zero deep in themselves.

The Point Zero Method

The Point Zero method is designed to free children from their fear to create and to fulfill their creative potential. The method addresses every aspect of children's fears and apprehensions and encourages them to find inspiration and answers within themselves. It deals with the *whole person;* it can bring struggling or uncreative children back to themselves and into their lives and feelings.

Children feel great pressure from demands and expectations to perform, and that pressure prevents the full working of their intuition. To meet their creative power, children need freedom in a structured and ordered environment that welcomes and understands the mystery and playfulness of creativity. In such a magical context they develop the capacity to reach the source of their intuition—Point Zero—and they learn to use it to create. With room to be spontaneous, they discover how to truly invent and develop authenticity and uniqueness in their work. They learn how to express themselves and explore their world using heartfelt energy.

When creativity is approached in the *traditional way,* making art requires special talent and aims at producing a masterpiece. That approach might develop some technique, but it does not work for the child's benefit. In it children must follow rules and create realistic images; creativity then is another subject to be learned with its demands and limitations, and they find in it very little freedom to invent, dream, and express. Parents often choose that approach because they can relate to realistic images and believe they see progress as the child learns practical techniques like perspective and texture. Unfortunately, that approach will pull children away from their creative inspiration because in it their spontaneity and intuition are barely used. The work is more oriented toward achieving than inventing. Creation becomes about acquiring a skill and is done within the pressures of success and failure. When art is taught this way, children create from their head, deciding and planning every move, always thinking of the outcome. No wonder so many children become discouraged! Very little room is given to their originality and creative potential. The sense of joy and adventure disappears as well as the precious possibility of self-expression.

However, if creativity is approached as a means to expressing feelings, then *making art requires spontaneity and freedom*. Pure creativity and self-expression go together. When children are free to follow their hearts in creation, they spontaneously express themselves. Feelings and emotions are stored inside the heart, but as soon as they are allowed to come out, they eagerly do. In spontaneous creation it happens automatically, as if feelings had been impatiently waiting for that opportunity. In a safe context intuition flows, and children let their feelings take the shapes and colors needed at the moment. The power and intelligence of creativity is such that it expresses what is most needed. Creativity brings balance and harmony in the lives of the young painters, relieves the pressures of growing up, and allows intuition to be an active power in life.

By offering children a conducive context to create, we help them find the source of their creativity. We need to keep in mind that *intuition* and *spontaneity* are the catalysts that put creativity in motion. We can guide children toward themselves by respecting the basic Point Zero creative principles:

- Creating for process, not product
- Using intuition and spontaneity as the fuel and fire of creation
- Banning criticism and evaluation as damaging to the child

The Point Zero method:

- Creates a context of safety
- Removes the pressure of performing
- Offers creative adventure and process
- Encourages spontaneous self-expression
- Inspires self-reliance at all times
- Respects each child's peculiar needs

It is possible for every child to experience the joy of creation when the right support and understanding are present. Creativity is a powerful force that can become an intricate part of a child's life if the child is properly introduced to it. Such an approach can lay the groundwork for a lifetime of creative passion.

Starting a Creative Painting Class

Children must feel that they are loved and appreciated for who they are, not for what they do.

—M C

When I taught my first class at a private school in San Francisco, I gathered the children in the middle of the painting studio. We sat on the floor in a circle. Lowering my voice, I spoke to them as if I were sharing a secret. I wanted them to know that painting in my class would be quite different from learning academic subjects. If they could realize that creativity was for their joy and self-expression rather than to accumulate knowledge and get grades, it would make our creative painting class buzz with excitement.

Our painting studio was a small rectangular room in the basement. The walls were covered with soft fiberboard for pinning up large sheets of paper to paint on. In the center of the room stood a painting table that displayed twenty colors, each one equipped with three brushes of different sizes. The children would paint standing up, moving back and forth to the central table. (For more on the setup, see chapter 5.)

"This studio is a very special place," I said. "Nobody else other than you and me is allowed here in this room. This place is

just for us. I will keep the paintings in the closet where nobody can criticize them or even see them afterward. We are in a private and secret place, and here you can paint anything you want without worrying. *I won't be giving grades, and we won't have any contests.* This place is truly magic!" Lowering my voice one more notch, I repeated, "This is going to be an adventure!"

I doubt that any of the ten children, aged six to eight, truly understood what I meant, but I had given them the message that the class was going to be special and that I was fully on their side.

The children seemed to be intrigued—afterward they talked to one another with the same low voice I had used, as if sharing their own secrets. A sense of mystery was already floating in the room.

We gathered around the painting table in the middle of the room, and I explained how to hold the brushes so they wouldn't get paint all over their fingers. I showed them the balance of water and paint that would work best. I insisted that they don't push too hard on the brush lest they hurt it. "Your brush gets thirsty really fast. You need to give it a drink of water often or it hurts!" I repeated slowly, looking into their eyes to make sure they heard me. "Never push too hard on a brush; you could ruin it in two minutes. You always must hold your brush very gently." I showed them a misused brush with the bristles broken at the base. "These brushes are very good, but they are fragile. You have to treat them gently."

"And now, everyone can start!" I announced cheerfully. "One, two, three, and GO!" I followed my words with a coaching gesture.

"What should I paint?" asked Melanie, suddenly paralyzed, a six-year-old with black velvet wide-open eyes.

"Yes!" echoed an excited Tom. "What do we paint today?"

"I never tell anyone what to paint, and I never give assignments for the whole class. It wouldn't be fun for you. You can
choose whatever you want. In this class we invent everything.
There are no mistakes."

Both children would have preferred getting directions because
they were so used to it, and in that moment they were feeling a little scared. But Stephanie, a taller girl in tight jeans and pink bulky
sneakers, boldly grabbed a brush and dipped it in yellow paint. She
went to her blank sheet of paper pinned to the wall and painted a
large sun in the middle of it. Another child followed her example,
and within a few minutes all children were painting.

I kept very busy showing each one, over and over again, how
to hold the brushes and how to dip them into water and paint. I
ran from one child to another trying to catch drips before they
went too far down or to pushpins before they popped out of the
walls. Within an hour we had become a team working together,
but each one in a private space.

It really does not matter in what way a class starts, as long as a sense
of freedom and intrigue is born. You, following your own inspiration, need to make sure you play the role of catalyst and guardian
of children's creativity and that you protect the space and bring
structure. Your main function is to *free* children from creative rules,
prejudices, and beliefs they have already absorbed.

Unfortunately, this is not always obvious to parents. Parents
often worry about their children. They ask, "Is my child talented?"
or "Is my child as good as others?"

For this reason, teachers might need to educate parents about
the true meaning and function of creativity, its quality of self-

expression and spontaneity. Often time has to be scheduled in advance for this purpose, so parents can feel comfortable and appreciative about their children's creativity and can fully support their creative process.

Parents and teachers need to stop worrying about talent and competition. They need to understand that the power of painting is not about winning a contest but about giving a precious tool to their children, a tool they can use for a happier, more integrated life. It is not what the children do in the painting studio that is important, it is how they open up and learn to respond, take risks, and listen to themselves. What is talent if not the courage to be oneself? Children want to be seen for who they are.

When the magical space is finally created, new children can join at any time. They find their freedom through osmosis. The painting studio, a womb for creativity, nurtures and protects the children while they grow up and explore their creative potential.

How the Creative Process Works

*Education consists mainly in what we
have unlearned.*

—MARK TWAIN

If we want children to use painting as a tool for self-expression
and self-discovery, we don't need to teach them technique.
On the contrary: we need to *unteach* it. *The less technique children
have, the more they use their intuition.* Technique overrides intuition.
As adults we should clear out unnecessary baggage for children's
freedom of creation to unfold. When painting they must be allowed
to follow the dictates of their intuition. Free from rules, they can
learn to paint images from deep inside and express what is unique
about themselves.

When at times a special technique is needed, technique spontaneously develops. Children invent or reinvent it. Their skill develops out of the intricate demands of their feelings, not from aesthetic
concepts. Whatever they paint is done with their whole being and
carries the stamp of authenticity and the beauty of their innocence.

The way each child perceives and senses the world is unique.
While the body and mind constantly grow, perceptions also change.
If children paint naturally, we can actually document the *evolution*
of their perceptions of the world. Their visual expressions of the
sensations of the human body, for instance, change constantly, if they

are not asked to copy models or respect proportions. For instance, the image of a person's head evolves spontaneously from very big (much bigger than the torso) to relatively small (close to standard proportion) within a few years. Every part of the body image goes through an evolution. Fingers, for instance, are first felt as long lines coming out of a circle. After a couple of years these five lines retract in length slowly to create fingers. Children must be encouraged to be spontaneous and to forget about the outcome by *spontaneously* expressing these differences and changes, which, in fact, they are not aware of.

Children's sense of the material world and of the space around it also changes. They perceive space in a special way. First, not knowing the relationship between ground and object, very young children often paint objects and people floating in space. Then the ground appears just as a brown line or leaves of grass (see painting 1) but later fills with dirt and grass (see painting 5). The sky often starts as a blue line and also expands slowly (see painting 16). If children are left free to paint intuitively, a fascinating process happens: the two lines—the one from the sky and the one from the earth—gradually move toward each other, slowly filling the gap between them. After a few months of spontaneous process, the space is finally conquered (see paintings 8, 9, 10). This final moment—when paint covers the *entire* space—is a very special moment. Watching that unique milestone always touches me greatly because the children have reached within themselves to a brand-new place; in it there is no return. It is a time *of initiation* for children, a precious stage in which space is inwardly conquered. This powerful event cannot take place if they are taught perspective and are depicting space in their paintings through rules and techniques. Children never regress in their evolution. They keep moving ahead.

A friend of mine has a ten-year-old boy. One day my friend

was discussing with his son, just back from a painting class, how his drawing had three-dimensional qualities. The father was marveling at it. The son, a stern look on his face, didn't seem to think there was anything exciting about having struggled two hours for a little bit of perspective while painting a wooden chair he didn't care about. He seemed impatient to move on to other things, saying, in effect, *I have worked hard enough, I deserve to play now.* After that class he never wanted to paint again. Having not touched his true creativity, how could he want to go back to it? Learning technique often alienates the child and presents creativity as work without much reward.

Perspective can be discovered spontaneously; children left to themselves come upon it bit by bit when the time is ripe. Painting in perspective becomes part of a natural instinct instead of a mental discipline; the resulting paintings breathe *aliveness* instead of the stiffness of those trying to do it right. Trying to paint right often ends with a painting that looks like a scientific study.

It's fascinating to watch the evolution of children's paintings. Look at a table, for instance. When young children paint a table, they paint its legs hanging in the air (see painting 14). Then, within a few months to a couple of years, the table legs slowly lower until one day they are set firmly on the ground. This also proves why children don't need technique if they are allowed to paint what they feel.

We must let children experience their world and create intuitively from their natural perceptions if they are to enter the magic of creativity. If we force children to paint with "normal'" proportions and with perspective, they *miss* an immense opportunity. They repress their intuition and grow up without much creativity.

Don't worry about the rendering of children's paintings. The creative process is a process of exploration, and it stays with them wherever they go. That process has an internal intelligence that guides them as they grow.

Process versus Product

Success can eliminate as many
options as failure.

—TOM ROBBINS

Children want to paint for themselves, not for others. When they are following the basic needs of their own expression, they don't need adults to tell them that the painting is good or beautiful. *Creativity is process,* and this is the message we want to give children. To give this message, we have to become aware that every time we evaluate their work, with a compliment or a criticism, we are taking them away from process and with it their freedom and power of invention. We make them self-conscious about their work, and they lose the magical space of creation. We strengthen their concern about the product, taking away the beauty of their journey into the unknown.

Diane, a shy and well-behaved ten-year-old girl, joined the painting class. She chose the most remote corner of the room to paint in and started working almost immediately. Half an hour into the session she called me over. "Michele, do you like my painting?" she asked with an insecure voice, showing me a yellow house she had just painted.

20

This one is for the refrigerator!

What adult wouldn't want to give that child what she asked? Wouldn't want to make her feel good and show her she cares? The natural response to such a question seems to be "Yes, I like it very much," to give encouragement and confidence to the child. The trouble is that in creativity it does not work that way. Compliments always backfire in the long run. *A good comment becomes a bad comment,* because praising the work puts the emphasis on the product instead of on the process. The child, liking the compliment, works to get *more* compliments and in doing so forgets the adventure of creation. Worried about doing something wrong, the child becomes afraid to be spontaneous and to explore the unknown, and soon the deep connection with heart and intuition is lost. When teachers or parents assess the work, the child, becoming aware of it, instinctively adopts the same attitudes and judgments and, sadly, becomes self-critical.

For the sake of the children we need to change our habitual response to their work and find other ways to nurture them. We should not be concerned only about giving them instant gratification but rather *long-term support* for the development of their creative potential. We must support the essence of creativity and the purity of its source by consistently bringing children's attention *back to process.* This attitude prohibits evaluative comments of any sort.

It is a very delicate thing to answer children in ways they do not wish or expect.

I looked deep into Diane's eyes and said, "I am sorry, I never answer that kind of question. Here we paint to explore and play. Nobody judges or grades the work."

She looked at me as if I were a creature from outer space. She opened her mouth, wanting to say something, to argue, but nothing came out.

Next painting she asked me again, "Michele, do you like my painting?" I smiled gently and said, "Diane, I am glad you painted that painting."

"I want to know how much you like it," she insisted with a faltering voice. "My mom and other people always tell me."

"I am sorry, Diane, but I don't think like that," I answered. "I was happy to see you painted every little bit of your painting. I don't either like it or dislike it."

She stayed there, confused, entangled in various thoughts, attempting to make sense of the situation, trying to understand a new way of looking at paintings from this strange French teacher.

Next session the same dialogue: "Michele, do you like my painting?" She asked me nervously three times, probably hoping that my old responses where just temporary mistakes and that I would eventually come back to the normal world.

By the third session she stopped asking. She became very quiet and concentrated. We talked of other things. She asked me how to mix paint to get the exact color for a sunset she wanted to make. She discovered ocher and said how it reminded her of the fall leaves on the East Coast. When she ran out of ideas I challenged her with a few questions: "What if something could pop in your painting all of a sudden?" and "What if something new could enter the painting from any side?" or "What if you took a small brush and see if it wants to add a little detail, a dot, a small line anywhere?" and she found a way to go on by herself.

She never asked again if I liked her work. And I got a strong feeling that by then she wouldn't have liked to hear about it, whether good or bad. There was so much more space for her that way. She had entered the world of spontaneous expression, and from then on nobody had any right to intrude in it. I supported her process, and that was enough. Diane had understood that creation is done for its own sake and found her creative passion. She was not ready to relinquish it for someone else's *irrelevant* opinion.

When the Creative Connection Is Cut

*Every child is an artist. The problem is
how to remain an artist once he grows up.*

—PABLO PICASSO

When children lose their desire to create, it means they
have received a message that killed their enthusiasm—
a judgment or a demand to *perform* that transformed
their creativity into work. That unfortunate interaction, that interference, was probably directed at something they had created full-
heartedly. Suddenly pulled out of the wonderful freedom and ease
of spontaneous creativity, they felt hurt and confused and started
doubting their spontaneity. This is a common experience for many
children. That defining interaction often happens when they are
still quite young—*at four, five, or six years old.*

From that point on, children believe creativity is another subject to struggle with, and they lose much of their enthusiasm and
attraction for it. Their natural spontaneous connection with creation as play and adventure is severed, and they simply turn away
from it.

Children will still "create" when adults ask them to, but they
will do it only for the outcome, to please and impress, always
wanting to be liked and appreciated. The true enjoyment of creation has vanished; the excitement of exploration and the passion

are absent. They go through the expected motions, but their hearts aren't in it.

The good news is that the connection can be reestablished. It can be done when children are put into a context in which creativity is given full respect and understanding. There they are gently guided to move away from product. Grades, criticisms, rewards, and punishments are banished. They are not expected to paint images realistically or to paint paintings that make sense to the adult mind; they are not asked to explain or justify what they created. They are on their own to decide what is to be done next and how to invent it. The results are as private as their journals would be, protected from anyone's comments. With the Point Zero method, adults develop an affectionate and understanding support but with no direct interference. In the right context (which I will discuss later), two weeks to two months may be needed to restimulate creative passion.

In an atmosphere of utter respect for the creative process, children reenter their dreamworld and become reacquainted with their intuition. When they reenter the creative space, a space where success and failure are absent, where feelings and intuition are free to be explored, they become whole again. The return to the source, to Point Zero, is a most significant event.

Parents

Grown-ups never understand anything by themselves, and it is exhausting for children to have to provide explanations over and over.

—ANTOINE DE SAINT-EXUPÉRY,
The Little Prince

Parents love their children and want the best for them. Yet it is hard for parents to be aware of the long-lasting consequences of their opinions and demands for their children's creativity. Their attitudes often determine their children's creativity as adults. As a teacher I often spent more time educating parents than teaching their children. I had to, to keep well-intentioned parents from undoing my work. Often adults can foster the creative element in children by dealing with their own creativity issues. It is a wonderful opportunity for them to explore and learn about their own lives as well as their children's. Creativity deals with the core of who we are and touches all aspects of life.

Children want to please their parents and are extremely sensitive to their attitudes, whether verbal or silent. Children have the uncanny ability to read their parents' feelings or thoughts. If parents fake a response, they know it instantly. Each parent, aware of it or not, has an opinion of what is a good or bad creation. The

one for dad...

One for me...

child is greatly impressed and conditioned by these expectations and judgments.

The saddest part is that parents' best intentions are often damaging because children need a safe but *understanding* space for their creativity to bloom. Very little is needed to take away a child's freedom of creation.

Parents' most *undesirable* attitudes are the following:

- Judging the work if the child does not paint
  realistically
- Systematically showering children with compliments
  and praise
- Looking at creativity as a means to produce nice art
  objects
- Showing children how to paint something
- Evaluating the work and suggesting changes
- Correcting or fixing children's paintings
- Comparing siblings' creativity
- Worrying about the meaning of painted images

Because parents have the power to stop children from finding their inspiration, the Point Zero method asks parents to be extremely careful not to interfere in the natural development of children's intuition. If parents want creative children, they must look at creativity as a unique tool for cutting a path to the heart and soul, not as a product-oriented activity. Parents must understand that creativity is a precious activity children can use during the sensitive years of growing up to find self-confidence, self-reliance, and fullness in themselves.

Parents and Teachers at Work *Part I*

*Let your insights and discoveries transform
your attitude. Let them teach you that
every dragon seen is half-conquered.*

— M C

YOUR PERSONAL WORK

Your attitude strongly influences the amount of creative freedom children have. Whether or not you talk to them about it, your beliefs and prejudices limit them. *Becoming aware* of your attitude will bring *insights* that will help you guide and support creativity. Here are some questions to help you discover how you truly look at the creative process and what you expect from it.

Take time to write out your answers. Seeing them in your own hand and exploring them on paper will guide you to your truth. Take all the time you need; the truth comes slowly. Explore your feelings, think about them, and then write some more.

Fourteen Questions
to Ask Yourself about Yourself

1. What are *my beliefs* about creativity? What do I really think about it?

2. How *do I feel* about my own creativity? What place do I give it in my life?

3. *What do I personally want* from children's creativity? What am I expecting?

4. What are *my* hopes, *my* demands, *my* preferences, *my* fears, and *my* agendas for children? Can I let myself see them?

5. What am I the most *attached to getting* from children?

6. Am I really *interested* in children becoming creative, or do I have other motives? Am I trying to fulfill a precise goal, or am I open to creativity's work?

7. Do I look at creativity as a *tool* to help children grow or as a hobby? Can I let myself feel the power of creativity?

8. If children do something unexpected or unusual, *will I judge them?* What are my limits?

9. Do I consider the expression of *sexuality or violence* taboo?

We are all critical in some way. What is important is to be aware of our prejudices and see how they affect the children.

Write down as many judgments as you possibly can. After you discover them, their power to limit children will diminish as well as their power to affect and limit *your own creativity*.

10. Do I bring to the child a sense of *competition,* and do I bring a sense of success and failure to creativity? You might not have been aware of it before now. Competing is a collective human pattern that might sneak up on you without your knowing it. When you're aware of this, you can see how much it must affect the child.

11. Do I believe that creative talent is only for *special* and rare children, or can I see creative potential in every child? How do

I really feel about talent? Do I judge my child as not being especially talented?

12. Am I truly interested in the *process* of creation, or do I mostly want beautiful *results* from it? Can I let myself see process, not just the resulting product?

13. How do I feel about spontaneous expression for *myself?* Do I know firsthand how it feels to express myself? Do I wish to find more of it in my life?

14. How do I feel about spontaneous expression for *my child?* Do I want a child who expresses feelings and concerns freely?

List your answers and revelations.

- See your personal investments as a teacher or a parent.
- See your beliefs as a creator.
- Bring yourself back to Point Zero, your personal source of creation.
- List the consequences of your attitudes and prejudices.
- Highlight the most crucial points.
- Remember that by doing the work you are getting to know yourself and your relationship with your children.
- List your *insights.*

EXAMPLES

Lisa's mother, a young, vivacious, intelligent mom, told me that after asking herself these questions she discovered that she

wanted Lisa to be successful in the art world because she loved beautiful things. She had always dreamed of painting but thought she was not good enough. She finally realized that she was putting great pressure on her daughter. She shared: "I thought I was inspiring her by telling her how to use and balance colors and images. I was wondering why she was so reticent to paint."

Robert's father told me, "I realized I didn't want my son to be completely immersed in the computer like I am. I made him paint to please me, not him. I wanted him to do great work in different areas."

Nadine had a class of six- and seven-year-old kids. She said, "When I questioned myself I saw that I was looking forward to the exhibit we had at the end of the year and wanted people to be impressed. I kept looking at aesthetic values."

June had her two children take the class. "I saw that I wanted them to compete. I thought it was good for them. I was pushing them to satisfy my own ambition."

Janine, a four-time mom, told me she had an insight: "I have always been afraid to create and wanted my children to succeed in it. I wanted them to *fight my fears.*"

Never feel bad about what you discover about your attitudes or prejudices. We all have judgments and vested interests underlying our behavior. Every realization can change your life for the better and with it your relationship with creativity and children.

35

Parents and Teachers at Work *Part II*

Education sows not seeds in you,

but makes your seeds grow.

—KAHLIL GIBRAN

YOUR WORK AS A FACILITATOR
OF THE CREATIVE PROCESS

The following questions will help you perceive fully children's underlying motivation to paint and to better understand their particular behavior while doing it. You should observe children at all times.

Nine Questions
to Ask Yourself about Children

1. Are children trying to *please me* by attempting to do what I expect?
2. Are they worried about *not doing well*, about not being talented enough?
3. Are they feeling unwilling or *uninspired?*
4. Are they *competing* and comparing with others?
5. Are they trying to use their paintings *to get MY attention?*
6. Are they using their paintings *to get someone else's attention?*
7. Are they afraid of being judged and *evaluated?*

8. Do they feel *adequate?*

9. Are they *free* to play and invent?

List your answers.

Answer all the questions as best you can. *While you are answering the questions, you are getting to know your children and their needs.* The more aware of children's feelings you become, the more powerful your guidance and support will be.

Put yourself in children's shoes.

- List the consequences of the attitudes you discover in yourself.
- Try to remember past interactions you had with children and their outcomes.

Often parents make comments that reveal their nonverbal demands and prejudices. If you pay attention, it will become obvious to you how these demands *pressure* children in their creative work. For instance:

"I want Jack to be good in the arts. His brother is good at sports, and he needs to be good at something too."

"Her sister does marvelous paintings. I want her to learn too."

"She draws a lot, but she does not know how to draw proportions."

"My son paints battles a lot. I would like him to do other things."

"I want my daughter to be able to make cards for Christmas."

"My father was an artist. I think he is too!"

If you pay attention to the statements you make about your children and their creativity, you will extract insights from each one.

Find more direct help by referring to the eleven guidelines for optimum creativity listed in chapter 5.

You might be surprised *how quickly* children respond to adults who try to meet them in their creative process. Children can adapt very fast to freedom and exploration when they are given the space. You will be delighted to watch the joy children will feel.

Intrusions to Creativity

*When they tell you to grow up, they mean
stop growing.*

—TOM ROBBINS

To create a magical context that fosters spontaneous inspiration and self-expression, parents and teachers need to become aware of possible intrusions into children's joyful processes. Commenting on children's paintings is extremely delicate and can be unknowingly threatening to a child.

It may not seem like it because these questions can feel natural, but here are the three basic intrusions to children's creativity:

Asking a child: "*What* did you paint?"
Asking a child: "*Why* did you paint that?"
Asking a child: "*Tell* me something about your
    painting."

Asking a child, "What is it?" is comparable to saying to the child: "I can't figure out what you tried to paint. Because I can't figure it out, it does not really work. You have failed in your representation." Children do not know that you cannot recognize what they created; to them their images are obvious and accurate. They naturally do not judge their work unless they have been conditioned to do it. The question "What is it?" always disappoints and saddens children, who later try to avoid such remarks by painting what is expected and by trying to reproduce images exactly, losing the joy and freedom to feel and invent. Although you may have good intentions, the question "What is it?" shows a *lack of respect* for the children's world. Your demand to label what they do instead of observe and appreciate is perceived as a denial of their reality.

Asking a child, "Why?" is very disturbing to the child. Children, being spontaneous, move through images as if in their dreamworld, flowing with the current of inspiration. In the truthfulness of their response to intuition they paint things they *cannot* explain. They paint what they could not express in words. For example, when Cathy's mother asked her, "Why didn't you paint a neck on the little girl?" Cathy could not give her a good reason and felt very bad. She just said in a pitiful tone, "I forgot." She had not painted necks on her people since she joined my class. It was her way of expressing her feelings about the body. She was naturally responding to her intuition, which is an integrative and harmonizing force. When her mother came to the studio and asked Cathy in a disturbed voice, "Why is it missing?" she took away her daughter's confidence in her spontaneous expression and with it stopped the *natural evolution* of her process. She set a barrier to Cathy's creative path by giving her the message that her intuition was not trustworthy.

Asking a child "Tell me" is asking a child to leave the nonverbal world so full of the potential of expression and to go into his or her head to satisfy the adult. It is a *major* interruption in the child's creative flow. Freedom, mystery, and spontaneous exploration are lost instantly. That question tempts the child to give adults what they want. Children will often make up stories to please adults and, sadly, abandon the adventurous process of their creation.

When children are truly ready because creativity has helped them move through their feelings, and when they want to talk, they will do so spontaneously.

Parents and teachers cannot gain trust or find valid information by asking children those three questions about their paintings because:

1. Whatever children paint is often not directly related to what is going on in their lives.
2. What is most important about the painting is hidden to the child.
3. What the child expresses CANNOT be told in words.
4. The *process* of creation affects the child more than the images and scenes that are coming out of it.

Children are more likely to open when we do not intrude in their work and keep a safe and understanding atmosphere. Often, when children share about their lives, their confidences are not directly related to the painted images, yet that unsolicited contact is always significant and gives us a springboard to being with them in a more intimate way.

Parents and teachers can support children best by allowing the nonverbal expression of creativity, with its *mystery* and *privacy.* In the following pages, you will find ideas and pointers to help you respond in the most efficient way when the situation seems to call for the *What, Why,* and *Tell Me.*

CHAPTER TWO

Creativity and
Self-Expression

This chapter will bring parents and teachers a greater *understanding* of creativity and its potential for self-expression.

It will also inspire and guide them to nurture their children's natural ability to create and to discover the amazing connection between *feelings, intuition,* and *creativity.*

Stories of children painting will illustrate how:

- **I**ntuition leads naturally to self-expression
- **S**elf-expression brings joy and passion to creativity
- **P**ainting skills develop spontaneously
- **C**reative blocks appear—and what to do about them

How Nicolas Found Painting Passion

When everything has to be right,

something isn't.

—STANISLAW LEC

Creativity is about children finding their own voice, the voice of their intuition. It is for them to express who they are and to explore their feelings and their world. It is also for them to discover that all they need to create is *inside* them—an unlimited source of inspiration—and that no matter what they want to express and create, *they can do it.*

When they realize the possibilities offered by creativity, their natural curiosity for discovery is stimulated. They quickly become more confident and intelligent in what they do. It is not the intelligence of the intellect developed through accumulating knowledge and facts, although that is affected too, but the spontaneous intelligence that directs their ability to respond and to grow, to become more healthy. They soon discover the power of self-expression and its joy, and with it their creative passion is born.

Nicolas, a dark-haired, bulky boy, was six and a half years old when he joined the painting studio, an after-school activity. His parents had registered him against his wishes. The first day he spent the session running to the window to watch with envy as other kids played ball in the noisy courtyard.

He asked me, "What should I paint?"

"You can paint whatever you want!" I answered in a fun voice, trying to entice him to create from his own world.

A few minutes later he had not touched his paper. "I can't think of anything," he said, dejected.

"Why don't you invent something?" I asked.

He looked back at me with a burdened face, utterly lost. Then he was still for a few moments, but I could see him thinking with all his might. He suddenly ran to the corridor and brought back a book he had in his backpack. "Oh! No!" I said. "Here we don't copy images from books; *we invent*. You can do it, too!"

Utterly disappointed, he gave me an unbelieving look. He was not prepared to create freely. He needed directions, guidelines, something to start with. I was asking him to do something that seemed impossible and that he couldn't understand.

Having no inclination regarding what to do, he waited and waited, feeling inadequate. That confusion was a defining moment because I left him alone to find his own way. He had *no other option* than to *rely on his own resources* without outside suggestions.

From the corner of my eye I watched him struggling with himself, looking for a way out. Twenty minutes elapsed while he stood there watching other kids paint. Then he got an "in-between" idea. Because he couldn't think of anything to paint, he decided to copy an older boy's painting. That was different from copying an image from a book. The other painter was involved in the creative process, and Nicolas was trying to follow his journey, to find inspiration through him.

He was now copying the other boy's work in a slow and uninterested way. I was happy he had made a small step.

Next session he arrived quite late and again copied the other boy's painting. One more session passed in the same fashion. The next time, when the other boy finished his painting, I quickly took it away and put it where Nicolas couldn't see it instead of letting it dry high on the wall. Nicolas, half-done with his painting, was now totally lost. He didn't complain, but it was obvious that he was getting quite upset. He had finally realized that he couldn't count on any help or tricks from outside. He had no other way out but to use himself. Suddenly, out of his frustration, he boldly scribbled over his painting with wild blue strokes and announced he was finished (see painting 4). During his scribbling, his feelings, though in a primitive form, had moved him for the first time. A direct contact between him and his creation had been born. This is when the creative shift happened.

As soon as he was done scribbling, Nicolas took a new sheet of paper. He carefully painted a dark brown tent with a red door, his first truly invented image. Then a picnic table appeared, and a sturdy tree, green grass, and a bright sun shining in the middle of it all (see painting 5). In just a few moments Nicolas's attitude had gone through a dramatic reversal. He had finally found a way to express himself. The magic of creation had started running in his blood.

"My family went camping last summer!" he volunteered to me with a radiant smile as he pointed to his brightly colored images. Then he painted a basket of fruit on the table.

As parents and teachers we should not be afraid to take away models and props, but we need to be clear about the reasons:

- Children have an infinite potential to create and
  need to *exercise* it.
- Children must practice relying *entirely* on themselves to
  find their own strength and power of self-expression.

47

Nicholas had found his own exciting play with painting. He had found *self-expression*. It was obvious how important painting then became for him. From that day on he arrived early to class. Eager to paint, he even helped me set up brushes and paints for other students. Happy and absorbed, he stopped running to the corridor to watch with envy other children in the courtyard. Nicolas had tapped into the source of creation and felt its endless possibilities. He now intended to use his newfound passion.

How David Discovered His
Painting Power

I don't paint things. I only paint the
difference between things.

—HENRI MATISSE

Children want to paint for themselves, not for others. If they are imitating or performing in order to please, their creations become work, and nothing really important can happen. But if children are following the basic needs of their own expression, they don't need adults to tell them what to do and certainly *not how to do it*. In a safe place and in the right context, children instinctively know how to proceed. They develop trust in their creative abilities and grow in originality and power of invention.

The painting class was ending, and I was helping children take off their aprons and find their school things while David finished his painting. David, a seven-year-old with an endearing smile and a vivacious personality, had painted a man in the middle of a large sheet of paper, big enough to fill the entire space. He was now hastily making blue buttons on the man's yellow shirt.

I happened to turn toward the door and was startled by what

I saw. *The man standing at the door was a replica of the man David had just painted.* The resemblance was so acute that I could barely believe what I saw. My eyes went from the painting to the man to the painting to the man in wonder. The resemblance was not only that David painted a tall blond man with blue eyes; he had captured a *feeling* about his father. David had painted from *inside* his feelings. Maybe it was the way the lip slightly slanted on the cheek or the way the eyes blurred around the pupils, or the slightly out-of-proportion head. I could not find what brought the acute resemblance. The answer was not on the material level, and it certainly had nothing to do with technique. The lively impact of this portrait came from another place. David had mysteriously grasped and expressed his father's presence. His spontaneous intuition had magically conveyed the essence of that man; the necessary skill had flowed through David freely as he gave himself to spontaneous self-expression.

I found out later that that was not an unusual occurrence. I made a game of guessing whose parents were whose by looking at the children's paintings. I was rarely wrong. So much for skill! I thought. What an intriguing phenomenon: the power of self-expression truly goes beyond technique! When feelings move the brush, feelings impregnate the work. Many artists, I am sure, would envy such perfect rendering.

How Joan Used Painting for
Self-Expression

*The heart has its reasons that reason
does not know.*

—BLAISE PASCAL

Spontaneous painting leads to self-expression. Self-expression in creation has an integrative effect that can be startling to watch. Any time children surrender to the creative force spontaneously, they flow with the current that runs through their intuition. Intuition is a force that not only allows children to play and create but also has a holistic effect. Deeply buried needs and longings reenter their lives through creation for greater fulfillment and integration. As in dreams, the intelligence of intuition guides children to experience and express what is most important for them at the moment. The same wisdom that generates dreams is at work helping children grow, integrate, explore, and heal in the joyful activity of painting. Joan's story had such a process. We, as parents and teachers, always have more to learn about and wonder at in the deep power of spontaneous expression.

Joan, a dark-haired six-year-old, carried a sense of secrecy about her. Thin, small, and restless, she had a lively personality but rarely looked me in the eye. When she came to the studio she didn't know what to paint. For the first few sessions she used her kindergarten repertory and reproduced designs she had learned there, scattering abstract shapes on the page without care. Constantly distracted, she talked to other children, ran around, and often left in a rush, with her painting apron still on. I didn't demand anything from her but that she didn't disturb other painters. She seemed surprised that I didn't tell her what to do or judge her for her behavior, or even demand that she accomplish anything.

Left to herself for a couple of weeks, Joan slowly quieted down while observing children paint. Something must have relaxed in her, because the intervals between her halfhearted attempts to paint shortened, until one day she was able to concentrate while painting a rainbow. We can follow every step of her spontaneous journey into creation in the series of paintings she made as if we were watching a movie (see paintings 6, 7, 8, 9, 10).

When she painted the rainbow, her restlessness disappeared and her guarded look softened. Soon her rainbow grew bigger, and, to my delight, she continued painting: a yellow sun in the left corner, lavender clouds, and birds in the sky. Finally, with a very tender gesture she filled the little *hollow* at the center of the rainbow (painting 6).

Then she started a new painting with the same image, and again when she was finished she filled the *center* of the rainbow, this time with gray paint (painting 7). She must have felt a stirring inside because she started to hum while she added small designs. During the next session, as if carried by a powerful instinct, Joan again painted a rainbow. With full concentration she carefully painted a small green tree in its center (painting 8). To my astonishment, the tree was pushing through the rainbow, filling *its hollow and striving for more space.*

In the following painting, her tree got too big to be contained in the little hollow of the rainbow (painting 9). *It broke through the rainbow* and kept growing and growing until it reached the sky. By that time Joan had found the source of her inspiration and kept following its current; the joy of creativity was moving her.

A week later the rainbow disappeared, but now nothing stopped the growth of her new tree (painting 10). She loaded it with red apples. She surrounded it with giant flowers, a picnic table, and birds. And finally, harboring a smile of fulfillment, she painted herself *on top of her tree.*

We may wonder what happened in the depth of her being. What dragon did she slay? What victory did she win? A little triangle squashed under the rainbow expanded and burst into freedom, her own freedom. Joan seemed to be *unaware of the evolution of her images* while they had unfolded. Inner work had taken place and healing happened while she followed her intuition. Joan had been at play. She had followed the mysterious streams that ran through her heart and found joy.

It is rare to have such a clear representation of a child's inner work; but no matter what is painted, when a child is free to express, the *same* process goes on. Parents and teachers should always keep in mind that fact. Knowing in their hearts the true purpose of creation will help them give children the support they need in letting the wisdom of creation do its mending and expanding work without their interference.

The Joy of Spontaneous Expression

Happiness belongs to those who are
sufficient unto themselves.

—ARTHUR SCHOPENHAUER

Children need to stop *worrying* about what they do. The pressure of doing it right can take over and prevent them from being creative.

Parents and teachers should support children in *finding their own way* naturally by listening inside themselves. When they are not told how to do something and not asked to follow ready-made tracks, they find inspiration spontaneously and learn to listen to their intuition. There is never a call for a model or a path to follow. Each creation is born out of children's needs and is unique in its expression. Creativity is experienced as pure play, and with that the joy and desire to create bloom.

"I don't know how to paint a person!'" cried Margaret, a worried, cute nine-year-old in a long brown dress covered with a multi-colored apron.

"Oh! I am glad you don't know how!" I exclaimed. "Then you can invent! Make it completely yours. I keep the paintings here in the closet like a secret. You can play and invent your own

54

without worrying about people criticizing them, and you can give your images any size, any shape, and any color. *You can paint, not to copy things as they look but to reinvent them and have fun doing it.* You can make a person any way you want. Okay?" I asked, looking in her doubting eyes. "I love painting people myself," I added. "I paint the arms as long as I want and the head any shape I want. Once I even painted a square one . . ."

She laughed then.

That's all that was needed: a sense of play about painting, not a sense of work or accomplishment.

"I want to paint a skyscraper but I don't know how to do it!" complained Victor, a robust nine-year-old boy who always filled his pockets with gadgets. He seemed quite restless; he must have had a difficult day at school.

"You can be your own architect! These days architects build all kinds of buildings. Some are even made with tires or beer cans, all sorts of sizes and shapes, and some are very strange. I am sure you must have seen some unusual ones. Why don't you invent your own? *You are the creator of your building and are allowed to do anything you want. It's fun to follow your fantasy,*" I told him with excitement.

He looked back at me with dull eyes.

"You can construct your own building. Can you imagine a special one?" I insisted. I had to talk to him for a few more minutes before he was willing to try.

Victor painted the most amazing modern-shaped building. Built on green posts, it had a round solarium station on top. Alien ships were circling around it. Victor was grinning with satisfaction. *He had found a way to enter his own world where there was no need for*

help and where nothing was missing. I was glad he didn't force himself to paint what he first thought he should do: a stereotypical building that had nothing to do with his present dream.

It is very revealing to witness children being afraid to explore on their own. It points to the fact that we have made our children dependent by constantly showing them and telling them how to proceed. In certain activities, like math or science, it is a necessary step, but it is very important to offer them *at least one* activity in which they can fend for themselves and find their way, an activity in which they can invent, express, and create freely. If we don't give them that option, they may become afraid or hesitant to experiment, and their creative spirit may fade away. Their only other choice would be to copy, repeat, or follow instructions but never to trust the immense possibilities of creation.

The Mystery of the Creative Instinct

*Pure creativity is a means for children
to grow and explore feelings.*

—MC

Play, self-expression, and creativity are tightly woven together and should be approached in that way. If allowed to express itself, the magic of creativity manifests in unthinkable and surprising ways, no matter the child's age or disposition. Creativity is an instinct; every child is born with the capacity and the urge to express and create. If nothing is done to stop that instinct, children fulfill that longing through intuitive play; often, the border between play and pure creation is invisible. That urge to create is not a random urge; it has its own natural order and direction, perfectly designed for the child's need for expression.

When my son, Philippe, was almost a year old, he would constantly manage to undo his shoelaces and take them out of his shoes. Then he loved to use the laces to make designs on the floor, which always looked like big drops of water (see illustration on page 59). He would systematically add something at the end of the shape, often with different-colored string or with whatever objects

he could gather. I kept wondering what pulled him to repeat that shape again and again.

When he became old enough to hold a pen, the first thing he drew was the same drop shape! And he used a second color to close the ending of it. For a few weeks he repeated the same form dozens of times in various sizes and colors, though there was a predominance of blue drops with red endings.

It was fascinating to witness such a young child carried by an urge to create so strongly that he had to invent ways to manifest it, using only what was at hand. I observed with wonder his intuition demanding true precision in his creation. I witnessed surprising resourcefulness in his constantly finding new materials to fulfill the mysterious urge to create.

Then one day the design disappeared, and I never saw it again—until a few weeks ago, when I sat down with my son's two-year-old daughter. The first form she drew was a shape that mysteriously was the exact same one as my son's first shape thirty years earlier; and she gave it an ending with another color.

The Dog Leaped Off the Painting

"Yes," I said to the little prince, "Whether it's a house or the stars or the desert, what makes them beautiful is invisible!"

—ANTOINE DE SAINT-EXUPÉRY,
The Little Prince

Why worry about the product and ask children to perfect their spontaneous creations? Why try to force them to match a projected outcome, an idea of beauty, a learned aesthetic standard? Creativity is there to naturally birth images, colors, and shapes; it feeds on life's juices and dreams. *We must learn to trust the infinite potential of all children.* Whatever they do, no points of reference could be relevant or could make any sense, because at every moment self-expression is unique. When the joy to create is present, a special energy moves children from deep inside, and we are left to marvel at the magic of creativity.

Peter, a quiet, soft-spoken six-year-old, an only child, took a big brush and dipped it in dark brown paint. He had just finished painting a heavy dark cloud and a puddle of blue water. Most of the lower part of the painting had been left undone. With complete confidence he went to that empty place and applied the brown paint. With his brush he quickly went back and forth a few times, covering a large part of that space. It didn't take more than one minute.

I thought he was scribbling. But then I watched him take some dark paint with a smaller brush and paint two black dots on the right part of the apparent brown blob.

As in a magic trick, suddenly a dog leaped off Peter's painting (see painting 3). It was so alive that I was taken aback. I could feel it breathe; I could see its long fur shimmering there on the wall. How could Peter create with such amazing liveliness and do it so quickly? I asked myself, stunned.

The brown dog was not just any dog; it was Peter's dog. And Peter loved his dog. With his whole being he had brought it to the studio to be with us.

Peter had attended my class for only a couple of months. He didn't use any techniques; he had not learned any. He just listened to intuition's urge and its mysterious inspiration. The currents of creativity birthed the dog naturally. Peter felt safe in his work. His feelings, his love for the dog, his joy, and his surrendering to intuition made the magic happen.

As adults we can help undo the conditioning that makes children create in the head rather than in the heart. Creation in the head holds no spark, no true contact or joy, because in it intuition and its mysterious power remain unused. Most children at four or five years of age already suffer from it. If Peter could enter his creativity in a couple of months and paint an amazingly lively dog in minutes, we can only dream of the immense and endless potential of pure creation.

The Enchantment of Creativity

It is not important to come out on top,
what matters is to be the one that
comes out alive.

—BERTOLT BRECHT

Creativity is very simple for children. It is just doing what interests them. But at first children who come to paint don't know what they want. They are afraid of not doing well; they want to know how or what to copy or imitate. They think the painting does not look good enough or realistic enough. They ask, "What is the color of the sky?" I tell them that there are many colors for the sky. I want them to invent everything, to reawaken their sense of play and discover the joy of self-expression. I make them discover that they are going to find all the answers inside themselves spontaneously. It is very important to put children in a position in which they rely on themselves and *at the same time feel completely safe*. It is the only way for them to enter more into their feelings, to express more of their world. Children have such an incredibly rich life; so many things happen to them, and so much needs to be expressed.

As parents and teachers we can offer children our trust in *who they are instead of what they do*. We need to feel totally confident that deep inside they know what to do and will find it. At difficult times we can remind them again and again of their capacity to face the unknown and invent. We need to inhabit the reality that creativity is in all of us, part of life's energy. The potential of children's creativity must be obvious to us. If we doubt their creative power, they will also.

Natalie was eight years old when she came to my painting class, a very thin girl with long, wavy blond hair and a worried face. She painted hesitantly, almost awkwardly, endlessly fixing her work. Not being able to come up with something of her own, she used the children's repertory of ready-made images, like bunnies and Christmas symbols, sadly copying stereotypical images stored in her memory.

One day she painted a large red cube, something she had studied in science class. After she had spent almost an hour struggling to draw the cube with proper perspective, she looked drained.

I approached her. "Natalie, what would you paint if you could really play without worrying about how it comes out?" She looked back at me with a serious and tired look. "What if you could stop worrying and let yourself invent in any way you want? That could be really fun!" I offered again cheerfully. This time she listened; I could sense something stirring in her. Then, I left her to her thoughts. A few minutes later she had painted two large pink hands reaching for the cube from the left side of the painting (see painting 11). The hands were painted in a bold and lively manner, quite a takeoff from her old way of painting. They were her first spontaneous images, a real breakthrough. She had finally let go of the thought of having to paint her image with "right" proportions and rendering; *she had freed herself from having to paint an image that was acceptable in the adult world*. Natalie had discovered that she could paint directly without planning and thinking so much. She could now relax and trust. Nobody would be judging her. She was finally safe and knew it.

That step, which took a lot of encouragement and a few weeks to occur, became for her a launching pad into the adventure of creation. A little later she painted her own room with a window dressed in green dotted curtains, a bed, a blue lamp, and other details (see painting 12). There was no more need for her to remember perspective or special technique. Natalie was joyful, radiant. She had come home to herself. She painted with tender care. From that day on her passion bloomed, and she kept inventing life scenes and dreamlands.

I'll never forget the day when Natalie painted the Golden Gate Bridge over the bay. She painted people standing under a lively sky watching an inflatable rubber boat (see painting 13). When she thought she was finished I talked to her. "Maybe a surprise is still waiting to happen; who knows?" I offered, trying to stimulate her to explore a little further. Part of my support to children is to stimulate their process at times. My purpose is to encourage children to feel that maybe they have not yet used their full potential. Stimulation should bring a sense of play, of space, of possibilities. By asking questions, we make children curious, and they become intrigued to continue the exciting journey of their painting. We have to do it in a sensitive and careful way because children should never feel forced. If they feel pressured or judged, our suggestions are refused and disappointment sets in. They should know that it is always *their choice* to add or not to add something to their painting.

I could sense Natalie was willing to search inside herself. She stood in front of the painting table for a moment, took bright yellow, and painted traces of sun among the clouds and the birds;

then she delicately put some touches of yellow on the bridge. She turned toward me. "These are small pieces of sunlight," she said, almost moved to tears by the beauty she felt in that instant. We both stayed silent for a while, enchanted, watching the sunlight gently touch the bridge.

Completing a Painting

What is this day with two suns

in the sky?

—RUMI

Children have a natural craving to express themselves. Painting for them is not just another subject to be learned. *It is a living process by which they move through events and feelings.* It has the quality of exploration; the suspense of what happens next is the enjoyment. As parents and teachers we want to make sure that children keep surprising themselves. Children enter the true adventure of creation when they learn to go to the end of what they start. To learn the art of completion they need to be guided not to be done with their paintings too quickly and to go as far as they can.

The ending of a painting is a very delicate time, because if the painting is left unfinished, enthusiasm and intuition will decrease for the following painting, and the momentum and the sense of adventure will dramatically fade away. *The further children go in their paintings, the deeper they will go in their expression and the happier they will be.* A barely sketched painting systematically brings discouragement, and soon the desire to stop painting sets in. On the other hand, when a painting is well completed, a sense of fulfillment and satisfaction arises and with it the inspiration for the next painting.

I am finished!

There are no models of what a completed painting looks like. It is always different, depending on the child and the timing. Parents and teachers can use their intuition and observe the children. After a while they learn to recognize the difference between the times when children have done all they could and when they just don't know what to do next and are trying to avoid going deeper, as sometimes all of us do.

When appropriate, we can help children by gently and playfully suggesting that mysterious possibilities might still happen. However, asking children to search for new ideas or details when they think they have done all they could think of is a sensitive interaction. Children might think their paintings are being judged, or they may feel pushed to do something they don't feel like doing.

Adults should always be aware of the nature of the creative cycle and its need for the completion of each painting. Here are some questions that can help this process (remember to always ask questions cheerfully and with a curious and interested tone of voice):

- "What would you do *next* if you kept playing and could do anything you want?"
- "Can anything *new* appear on your painting? A new idea can come all at once, out of nowhere! Can you look for one?"
- "So much has already happened! What would you do if you kept *inventing* and inventing? I wonder . . ."
- "Sometimes big surprises can happen at the very end. Can you check if one is coming?"
- "Could you check if a small brush could still paint something on your painting, maybe just a detail somewhere or even a dot or just a trace of paint?"

- "I wonder if you could squeeze out of your head *three more* things to paint?"
- "Can you take a brush with any color you want and see if the *brush* wants to paint something? Sometimes brushes paint on their own."

Questions should never bring pressure, but rather curiosity, a little like a game, as young painters search within for the last possible details or images. *That inward look stretches the creative potential and wakes latent resources.* New ideas are put in motion that allow children to create beyond the obvious, tapping into a level of feeling unknown to them. Passion grows.

Christine, an adorable five-year-old, called me over. "I am done," she said. "I need a new sheet of paper." Her painting, a beach scene, had a few images in pastel colors scattered around the page. I sensed there was more she could do.

"Are you sure?" I asked. "Maybe you could paint a little more on it."

"I can't think of anything else!" she said, matter-of-factly.

So I invented a game to inspire her to go to the end of what she was capable of doing. I gently put my hands on her hair and told her, "When I press on your head you might get a new idea. It's magic. Pay attention, I am right now squeezing ideas out of your brain. It always works."

She smiled back, doubting but willing to play. I applied very soft pressure to her head. "I am not getting anything," she said. I played along and very, very slightly I increased the pressure. I waited. Within fifteen seconds she exclaimed, "That's it! I got it! I got it! I am going to paint sand on the beach!" marveling at the magic of inspiration. And with the most careful brushstrokes she painted a multitude of grains of sand along the bottom of her painting, taking almost half an hour to complete. Then, a sudden new inspiration struck her: a series of variously shaped shells lying on the sand.

Christine was beaming. She had reached deep in herself and had found a ground that supported all her beach images. By not giving up and by searching deep in her intuition, she had found the source of her creativity. Point Zero with its inspiration had brought her creation to fullness. We looked at each other, and her happiness warmed my heart. I thanked the creative process.

Understanding Children's Creative Blocks

The water in your jug is brackish and low
Smash the jug and come to the water.

—RUMI

Like adults, children experience creative blocks. They are very common and can start as early as four years old. When children feel blocked, they lose interest in creation and generally ask adults to tell them what to do. They believe they need to be shown how to paint or draw and insist that you give them a model to copy or an idea of what to paint. Unable to express themselves and lacking enthusiasm, these children are afraid to be left on their own; creation has become a chore to them. When a child asks, "Tell me what to paint," *it's a sure sign of a creative block.*

Blocked children can't find ways to express themselves; to compensate they work at achieving something beautiful and attempt to get a reward by pleasing adults. When children are disconnected from their intuitive approach, they create with their heads, as mental exercises. They create in a mechanical way and think they need adults' guidelines, inspiration, and feedback.

Fortunately, this regrettable situation can be *reversed.* We can help children come back to themselves and recover their passion before it is buried too deeply.

The teacher just ruined my painting!

Children's creative blocks have different causes:

- Adults demanding a certain product (pressure for success)
- Children given models when they create (no spontaneity or self-expression)
- Adults asking them to develop painting skills (no freedom)
- Negative or positive comments made on their work (being evaluated and criticized)
- Lack of self-confidence (no connection with intuition)
- Having difficult feelings to express (emotionally overwhelmed)

We need to *become aware of what caused the block* and work toward freeing the child. This awareness develops as we discover more and more about the process and learn to observe the child from a place of understanding.

I often hear heart-wrenching stories from people, now middle-aged, who have stopped creating because of a demand or a single comment criticizing their work when they were little. If adults knew the impact of their unfortunate words or their well-meaning but inappropriate comments, they would be very careful.

Questions to Ask When
Children Are Blocked

What saves a man is to take a step.

Then another step.

—ANTOINE DE SAINT-EXUPÉRY

There are ways to stimulate and encourage children's creativity when it is sluggish or repressed. Our role is to help children find inspiration within themselves by stimulating play and expression and by helping them trust intuition and abandon criticism. Suggestions should never be made to paint certain images or shapes. Children should not be told how to paint. I don't think it could ever help them in the long run, and it may damage their instinct and ability to reach Point Zero. If children are told what to do, they cannot follow their intuition with its specific needs, proportions, colors, and images. *Intuition alone should dictate what to paint*. If children are asked to paint a tree or an apple, they may be able to put a little bit of themselves in it, but so little. It would feel like painting in a cramped space. If they are then told how to proceed to get special results, no room is left for intuition, spontaneity, and self-expression. Painting, then, becomes an exercise, a work to carry out within strict boundaries.

To bring children back to painting from their feelings, we

need to guide them by pointing *away* from traditional expectations and by focusing their attention on Point Zero and the freedom to express.

Here are some examples of questions we can ask; they are aimed at freeing children's minds from paralyzing ideas, like "I can't think of anything to paint!" or "I have made a mistake!" or "I can't paint!" These questions speak *directly* to the feelings, wake them up, and help spontaneous inspiration to arise.

- "What would you paint if you could really *play* without worrying about how it will turn out?"
- "This class is about inventing because it is *fun* and interesting. That's all. Do you want an adventure?"
- "Here we don't compete; we paint for ourselves. Do you want to try?"
- "I want you to feel you *can* do anything you want. I promise nobody will criticize you. *I know you are able to paint anything you choose.*"
- "These paintings are secret; nobody needs to see them. What would you paint if you could keep yours a secret?"
- "What would you do if you didn't care if the result was good or not?"
- "If you can't think of anything big, why don't you paint something small? Or the reverse?"
- "I know you feel that you are done, but if you think of something more it could become quite interesting. It's like a *game.* Can you find the next thing, small or big, just to *dare?* And maybe . . . one more thing after that?"

- "Could you take a brush, put any color you want on it and see if that color wants to paint something on your painting? Sometimes colors do! That would be a surprise, wouldn't it?" (This is a *very powerful and safe question* that can be asked as *often* as needed and in any circumstance.)

Spontaneity is the key to children's inspiration; therefore, they need to be taught to *take risks* and to trust themselves. Our silent but *constant* acknowledgment of their creative journeys brings them back to their hearts and gives them the necessary energy. Our understanding and awareness of their process make them realize when they are not truly using themselves. Our presence and contact become an unending reminder of how powerful they are when they use their intuition and let themselves invent.

When children come from an authentic place, our gentle enthusiasm and support (not through words but through eye contact) help them strengthen their creative power and self-confidence. Our attitude makes children feel seen and understood. They soon realize that no compromise would work as well as being true to themselves.

For instance, if children reproduce stereotyped images from books or magazines, they sense that it clashes with the energy of freedom and exploration in the studio. They also can tell I am not especially interested in their copying these materials, which makes them question their own interest. When their creative blocks finally break, I am fully there with them, present and appreciative. Slowly they learn to discriminate and understand the difference between paintings from their heads or their hearts.

With or without our questions, *children must find their own way by themselves.* The questions we ask them must address their inner world and *never* aim at one particular place or subject in the painting. Children are then brought back to Point Zero, the original place of creation that has no agenda. From that place of "everything is possible," children feel the stirring of what is important to them. Their feelings inspire them to respond. True inspiration is born, and creative passion returns.

The Healing Power of
Creative Expression

By trusting the creative process to bring
harmony in our lives we are trusting
life itself.

— M C

Creativity has healing power. An emotional wound, whether conscious or unconscious, is an aching place frozen in time. When children create, a life current passes through their being and instinctively meets the unhealed wounds. When energy reenters the frozen areas, spontaneous expression takes place. Through self-expression the sorrowful past events have a chance to finish their cycle, and healing starts. Understanding and acceptance of the heart often accompany that type of healing, which can't help but unfold in the little painters.

When parents and teachers become aware of the *intelligence* of the creative process, their attitudes toward it drastically change. They develop deep respect for the uncanny spontaneity of children and learn to observe rather than interfere in their creative endeavors. Parents and teachers can then rejoice in rather than worry about the bold or mysterious steps children take.

Why is creativity so powerful that it can heal deep wounds, unknown to the child or the parents? The answer is simple: it is because of the magical power of intuition. Intuition comes from the whole person, from a place that includes the conscious and the unconscious. The total result of all feelings and perceptions manifests spontaneously through intuition. *Intuition gives expression to the feelings;* that expression is unique and perfectly fitted to the needs of the moment. Spontaneous creation acts as a balancing and harmonizing principle. Deeply buried feelings come to the surface in a gentle way; their disturbing energies are diffused or transformed through self-expression. Painful feelings and sharp edges are smoothed; inner pressures are released. Children, freed from having to keep their pain in control, experience a joy and an aliveness that changes their lives. The heart, having its needs met, feels full.

When children enter the creative process their behavior toward siblings, friends, and parents changes in a positive way. Being more open, they have more energy and do better at school; having more space in themselves, they are more interested in learning and are more capable.

It is all very simple: When children truly create, they surrender to the *wisdom* of their own being, which knows what is good for them and what needs to be expressed. It all happens spontaneously when the right understanding and context are offered to them.

When the body suffers a wound, the body in time repairs the damage. In the same way, when the heart is bruised, creativity is the intuitive balm that brings healing.

How Brian Expressed His Feelings

Let my hidden weeping arise and blossom.

—RAINER MARIA RILKE

Difficult feelings are bound to come up from time to time in children's lives. Sometimes children come to the studio feeling overwhelmed by events happening at home, such as a divorce, sickness, parental stress, or by their own struggles in school or with their friends or siblings. During these times painting can be a wonderful tool to help the transition. Self-expression can have a powerful healing effect on children. These hard times are actually important, because children's sense of themselves is striving to be born, to integrate, and to heal. I encourage children to keep painting through them, to dig further into their hearts until there is an opening and release comes. Through their creative process they reveal themselves to themselves, and become whole again.

Brian, a nine-year-old boy, was shy and withdrawn. He had come from the Middle East and had just moved to San Francisco with his large family of nine siblings. He spoke very little English. Big for his age and a little overweight, he went timidly to a remote corner of the studio to paint. I brought him a painting apron and a sheet of paper, attempting to explain to him with my hands that he could paint whatever he wanted. He anxiously watched other children paint for at least ten minutes before he allowed himself to even pick a paintbrush.

Then he started. Slowly and sadly, he painted a big ocean, covering the bottom half of his large paper with shades of blue. When finished, he sat for a long time on a wooden stool, looking depressed. When he got up I saw him search for the smallest brush he could find and dip it into black paint. He painted a boy drowning in the immensity of the water. Then, a silent scream came out of him and he spelled the word *HELP* a couple of times in big black letters above the drowning boy (see painting 21). Brian had just found a way to express the intensity of his disarray. In that very instant a healing shift happened; the dark cloud that had surrounded him lifted and his face relaxed. Soon he painted a bright sun; then for the first time that afternoon, he turned toward me, our eyes met, and he softly smiled. There was no more need for language.

Brian had absorbed the sense of freedom and self-expression floating in the room. He had joined the class in the middle of the term; the other children were already involved in the creative process. He had felt the permission and the encouragement to be himself. It is always very helpful for newcomers to enter such a safe and concentrated place of creation. *Osmosis is a powerful force in a studio.*

Through his creative journey, Brian had begun to face the difficult state of being lost and overwhelmed and had found self-expression. Spontaneous images had moved out of his chest onto the paper, and now there was a bigger space inside him. In a foreign country he had made a connection with himself and had found a little space to stand on.

When children allow feelings to surface, they enter a healing process. Their feelings actually move from *inside to outside*. What is most difficult about painful feelings is that they contract and harden while we try to protect ourselves from them. When creation happens, the defenses that keep control over the feelings let down and feelings spontaneously express themselves, bringing release and integration. Feelings find room to be. The pain is felt but with space around it, because the contraction around it vanishes and *the pain can finish its cycle.*

Quite often gentle feelings follow self-expression and children volunteer a few words about what they just experienced or remembered. They sense their place in the world again; they feel they belong.

CHAPTER THREE

Creativity as Adventure and Exploration

This chapter will guide parents and teachers to support children in exploring their world with creativity. They will discover that the creative process is:

- **A** tool for spontaneous exploration and risk taking
- **A** means to go into the mysterious unknown
- **A**n intelligent and benevolent force that brings harmony and integration in children's lives

This chapter also discusses the *interpretation* of children's paintings.

Creative Adventure and Risk Taking

Only those who will risk going too far can possibly find out how far one can go.

—T. S. ELIOT

One of my roles as a teacher of the creative process is to ignite a sense of creative *adventure* in children. I delight in showing them the excitement of risk taking and the continuous *suspense* of creativity. The risks I ask them to take are about being spontaneous and about not censoring their inspiration. As parents and teachers, our work is to instill in children enough self-confidence to inspire them to trust their original instincts to explore and to *enter the vast unknown*. Each new step brings a surprise that comes right out of their being. What a wonderful feeling that is, to birth the unexpected!

The first painting session with a new group of children is often very noisy. Children, afraid to take the risk of being themselves, do not dive immediately into the adventure of creation. They bombard me with a wide array of questions: "Could you show me how to paint a fish?" "I don't know how to paint the water!" "What color is the sunset?" "Show me how to make a cat!" "What should I paint next?" And on and on.

Children generally don't trust their ability to explore and don't know how to enter the mysterious world of creation. Unfortunately, in their young minds they believe that to create is to reproduce something, not to *reinvent* it.

I told Annie, "All sorts of fish exist in the world, all shapes and all colors. You wouldn't believe how different they can be. Invent your own, you can't go wrong, take a risk! Dare to paint your own fish!" A few minutes later Annie had painted a wonderful fluorescent fish with a huge head and a little green tail. If I had shown her how to paint a fish, I would have taken away from her the delight of inventing. She would have missed the *adventure* of creation, its liveliness and its magic.

When Rick, an eight-year-old, asked me how to paint the sea, I told him, "The waters of the sea could be any color. The color depends on the light and on what minerals are in the water. Therefore, you can invent what you feel like. *Anything is possible!* It is up to you to experiment and take the risk to explore in your own way!"

My role as teacher is to make children understand that in their creation they can do anything that is natural to them. When creating, children enter their own world, and they should not be asked to follow suggestions but to listen to what their intuition wants. Creativity is the one place where no compromise should be made so authentic exploration can arise.

Creativity offers children all the space they need to form, color, and express their world. When they first make contact with that possibility they often feel overwhelmed and sometimes frightened by the vast potential it offers. Not used to the freedom to explore, they don't feel safe and need time and support to reclaim and recover trust in themselves. But, in fact, responding to their natural urge to explore is not actually taking a risk; the true risk would be in *not* following it.

A few minutes later, Rick had painted purple water with white-green foam and looked pretty pleased with himself. Why should the water be blue in Rick's dreamworld? Truly he was the only one to know. And Jean painted a brown sunset with yellow lines. It was perfect for what she was feeling.

When little Henry asked me, "How do I paint a cat?" I knelt down to be at his level and said, "Henry, do you realize how fun it would be to invent your own cat? A special cat, not like anybody else's cat." He looked at me with a puzzled and insecure look. But a few minutes later he had painted with abandon a yellow cat with green eyes. The proportions were awkward, but his spontaneous design gave it liveliness and a presence that touched the heart.

When he was finished he looked at me, and when our eyes met I saw that we had become friends. I had not asked him to come into *my* world; I had gone into *his*.

The Multiplying Volcano

*And the trouble is, if you don't risk
anything, you risk even more.*

—ERICA JONG

Often in a painting studio intense images like volcanoes, storms with lightning, earthquakes, and explosions spread naturally among the children. With this a sense of adventure and exploration is stimulated, and the desire to paint such images can become widely contagious. Children attracted by such power want to experience it for themselves. It has nothing to do with copying, and children should be allowed to do it.

When children respond inwardly to another child's painting, it means that the painting is touching a lively place inside them; *that painting is already in their inner world*, waiting to be born. Seeing it is only a reminder. Let them follow their spontaneous urge and let them explore it in their own way. It is never a cop-out but is a genuine response that deserves respect and support.

"Michele! What's the color of burning lava?" asked William loudly from across the studio. He was an outgoing boy, a quick-witted eight-year-old who after three painting sessions had finally found inspiration and was now painting a red volcano with a dark, deep crater.

I ran to his side. "William, don't scream like that across the room! You are disturbing other painters. What do you think the color of burning lava could be?" I asked, returning the question for his own creativity to answer. *Returning* questions is a safe way to encourage children to look inside and explore ways to answer them.

"I thought it could be red and yellow like fire, but I am not sure because ashes come out of the volcano too."

"And what color could the ashes be?" I questioned, asking him again to find his own answer.

Without a pause he replied, "Brown and black!"

"So, you know what to do!" I happily commented.

It's interesting how often children ask for what they already know. They ask as a way to make sure they won't get into trouble if they listen to themselves. William put a big blob of red paint on a large brush and with large gestures painted burning lava shooting up to the sky. He was grinning with excitement the whole time.

"Michele, Michele!" exclaimed Sophie, a few minutes later, totally outraged. "Jennie is *copying* William's volcano!"

I looked into her eyes and said without a trace of emotion, "So, what?"

"But . . . but . . . I thought . . . We shouldn't copy," insisted Sophie.

"Why not? You can use any image you want. Images belong to everyone. You can copy anything you like. Jennie liked the volcano and is now painting her very own. *She is creating a new one for herself.*"

When Nicolas was copying because he had no other idea (see chapter 2), it was a very different kind of action. He did it just to get by, mechanically. Jennie, on the other hand, was responding to her feelings and had a strong desire to paint a volcano. She painted it with such abandon. Seeing it must have awakened a feeling that was waiting for a long time. William's volcano had inspired her. She was truly exploring.

Puzzled, Sophie returned to her painting without another word.

Fifteen minutes later, oh! Surprise! A little volcano appeared in her painting. "Well done!" I thought, and I rejoiced at how fast she could drop a rule that didn't make any sense.

By the end of class, six more volcanoes had erupted in my small painting studio, all of them with different shapes and colors. A burning sense of adventure and exploration had suddenly spread among the little painters.

Fighting the Invasion of Stereotypes

We forfeit three-fourths of ourselves
in order to be like other people.

—ARTHUR SCHOPENHAUER

Often children coming to my painting classes have already lost their creative spontaneity. They paint by reproducing stereotypical images they remember. They cannot think of anything else to do and believe that painting a character or cartoon will be fun. There may be a small satisfaction coming out of mastering the reproduction of an image, but compared to the joy of self-expression and the freedom to explore, it is a very small reward indeed!

Copying is tedious work that tires children quickly because in it their creativity is not moving. It is very sad to watch children use their store of ready-made characters as if they had no source of inspiration from themselves. Most often they are not truly inspired to paint the superheroes; if they were, they would reinvent them from the inside and make them theirs instead of struggling trying to achieve resemblance.

When copying happens, parents and teachers need to bring children back to themselves and show them that creation is an ongoing adventure. They should nurture self-exploration at all costs; they must *avoid* offering the crutches of ready-made images and always encourage children to paint from inside. To discover creative passion, children must learn to track Point Zero within themselves.

"What time is it?" Jack asked me again, impatient for the class to be over. Jack, a handsome and athletic nine-year-old boy who always carried a heavy backpack, had joined the studio but without enthusiasm. When he found out that I didn't have models to paint from, he became quite upset. He had no idea what to paint and didn't trust himself to invent. Painting felt to him like another language to learn, a challenge he would rather avoid. So, despite my gentle summons, he kept sneaking into the hallway to peek at his comic books and copy from them. He usually settled for stereotypical characters like those from "Superman" or "Peanuts," and rendering these comic figures was hard work.

Where was Jack's creative passion? For years he had been told what to do and how to do it. His urge to invent and express was deeply repressed or even gone.

Would he get a second chance? Could he still discover the magic of his intuition? Or would the invasion of stereotypical images take over his attempts to create?

Jack needed time to shed his conditioning. He needed to experience freedom and its possibilities. He didn't know the amazing potential that lived in him, and to be asked to invent was an unwelcome request.

Every week I worried that he wouldn't come back to my class. By the fourth session, a bored Jack was disturbing his fellow painters by making funny comments and moving around the room. I had to interfere.

"It's okay with me if you don't want to paint," I told him, "but I cannot let you prevent the other children from painting. I want you to sit on a stool until the end of class and be quiet."

Jack sat there, surprised that I didn't compel him to paint. He started to watch other children and became curious. In front of him a boy was pretty excited painting a war scene; guns were firing over the hills and a silver cannon was shooting red and orange explosions into the sky. Jack became mesmerized. Some of that playful energy must have rubbed off on him because a few minutes later he asked, "Can I paint now?"

"Yes," I said, delighted to hear some excitement in his voice. I gave him a fresh sheet of paper.

Jack painted his own scene of destruction: a shark blowing apart a little boat floating on a big ocean and throwing the only passenger into the air (see painting 19). He stayed late to finish it, then left, a wild smile on his face. He had for the first time found the giving source of creation. By observing other children truly create, he had broken the belief that painting was tiresome work of reproduction that needed special talent. In the class he had slowly absorbed some of the exciting energy of creation. He could now use it; his desire to explore was enough.

Sometimes children must first experience the place of noninspiration and stay there awhile. Adults should *never force* a child to paint, but observe and be patient. Children shouldn't be rushed into filling their paper with anything in reach. From that empty and waiting place, creativity will wake.

Children's Custom-Made Images

The real voyage of discovery consists not in seeking new landscapes but in having new eyes.

—MARCEL PROUST

When children create from Point Zero, they wander into the wild land of their inner world; they become explorers. When not stopped by rules, they joyfully invent new proportions to the images they make. With a sense of no limit to what can be done, their inspiration births unique images and endless combinations.

Children express an intimate world that molds and reshapes itself, depending on their inner needs. It is *natural* for them to paint or draw out of proportion and not even notice it. For them it is the only way it can be: the representation is perfect and in harmony with themselves. The parts that are out of proportion, in fact, are the *most important* parts of their creation because in it everything is invented and intuitive. The free use of proportion is a tool that allows the expression of special feelings; it allows children to roam into the unknown and truly explore.

Each creation has its own shape and color. It must be kept that way. Children should never be asked to paint realistically. It cannot work for their benefit or for the development of their creativity. If they strive to paint realistically, their needs of the moment are bypassed and, sadly, true expression is blocked; they stop *sensing* and responding naturally. When painting realistically they go into their heads trying to figure out how to do it and struggle with rules and technique. This realistic approach is quite opposite to spontaneous creation, which is to enter joyfully in a virgin territory, a place without boundaries.

When Juliet painted a huge bowl on a table, she was not bothered in the least by the original disparity of her representations (see painting 15); when Amy painted people as tall as trees or the size of flowers, she was wandering in a private space (see painting 16).

The proportions children paint are never random. They are dictated by their intuition, *custom-made* by them. If adults ask them to paint differently, that demand violates children's creativity and discourages them from creative work. It ends up robbing children of the amazing adventure of creation. Children need to explore their world on their *own* terms; their intuition needs to spontaneously decide how big the dog, the head, the man, and the house are. The discrepancy of proportion is something to *rejoice* about. It's proof that children are true to their intuition, free in their spirit and adventure.

When children create, they need parents and teachers to fully trust and respect what they do. Every image is made anew, reborn anytime it is painted; it should stand on its own and be appreciated for the unique qualities that make it different from the traditional mold.

1

2

3

4

5

7

10

11

12

13

14

15

16

17

18

19

20

21

22

23

24

25

Interpretation of Images

An image is what it is, plus

ninety percent more.

—M C

The temptation to interpret our children's paintings is considerable. We want to find out more about their inner lives and help them; their paintings seem to offer such a possibility. This is a very natural response, yet it is not that simple. We need to inquire into the full meaning of creativity before drawing any conclusions about the content of children's paintings.

Young children spontaneously paint scenes from their lives, their fantasies, their dreams, and their nightmares. What can be seen in these images often is only the surface of their feelings; what is most important is often hidden or invisible and is *rarely depicted literally.*

Furthermore, we must keep in mind that a *child's process is always more important than what the painting shows.* The deepest expression of children's lives manifests in the doing of the painting through the magic of the creative process. As they paint different layers of their feelings, their psyches start to move. Children open up and explore their fears, their joys, and their thoughts; most of it happens instinctively. When intuition moves, it reaches deep into their hearts and souls and the natural intelligence of creation

What is wrong with him?

guides them. During this process children integrate events from their lives, and their emotions are *spontaneously* soothed; feeling better, they develop self-confidence and regain a sense of harmony and security in their lives. This is where the transformation of creativity happens—in that creative response. Transformation and evolution are not necessarily stored in the images or their interpretations; these processes move much *beyond* the page and envelop the entire child.

Parents and teachers need to keep in mind that *every painting is part of a whole* and is only a visual frame in the unending movie of their children's inner lives. Everything painted is evolving and transforming. If children are left free to create, their deeper self keeps emerging with its own rhythm, timing, and spontaneous revelations.

Instead of dissecting and explaining the paintings, we need to focus on how happy the children are. Are they changing? Do they sleep better? Are they getting along with their siblings and friends? Is their behavior improving at school? Do they listen more to what they are told? Do they learn better? When children truly explore creatively, this is where the clues are and where we can expect changes.

In rare cases, when children have emotional problems that require special professional attention, they volunteer a variety of clues through their behavior. This concern aside, we have to step back from the literal interpretation of the paintings and let ourselves be cradled in the mystery of form, color, and image. *We must respond to the child's process, not to content.* Children's paintings are like dream images, bathed in mystery. Images are what they are, and a lot more. I recommend that children be left undisturbed to do their work spontaneously.

Parents and teachers should never fear what has been painted lest they envelop children with their worries and divert or stop the current of self-exploration. Everything painted is on its way out; it is back into the movement of life, passing through the child, doing its harmonizing work. The intelligence of creativity does the healing. It is best not to interfere.

Death and the Apple Tree

*Art is a microscope which the artist fixes
on the secrets of his soul, and shows
to people these secrets which are
common to all.*

—LEO TOLSTOY

Children, like adults, have an urge to understand and explore the world. It is a great mystery to them, and they quickly realize that adults do not have all the answers. Creativity can then become a wonderful tool *to enter the unexplained areas of their lives,* a tool that can help them find their own answers to what preoccupies or intrigues them. During these times of exploration, children need full permission and understanding from adults lest they repress their feelings and deny themselves their needs. It is not always easy for a parent not to worry about painted images of death, violence, or sexuality. Often these areas are taboo.

You can feel at ease about these subjects. Emotionally healthy children have a tendency to be bold and daring in their freedom and paint these images whenever they feel an urge. If adults insist on worrying, better to worry about what children are *not* letting themselves paint, not about what they do paint. What needs to be painted and is not stays inside and turns around, creating disturbances. What is painted is back in the river of life and is on its way to be integrated or overcome.

When I saw Michael paint a grave in the middle of his painting, I watched him with great curiosity. He was just six years old, a vivacious boy with short, curly brown hair. Painting for him had been just another school subject, an unwelcome obstacle to playing ball with his friends.

Restless and barely able to keep his attention on his work, he spent the first sessions reproducing from memory comic book images. But today he was painting a grave, and this was not a stereotype. The image came right from inside him and took him by surprise. While painting he attempted to hide the daring death image with his body by standing very close to it. He was anxious and avoided looking at me. Had he gone too far? he wondered.

I behaved as if nothing special were happening. Michael painted two more graves, still glancing at me once in a while to make sure he was safe. After some time passed he seemed to relax and followed his intuition freely by painting more graves and a cemetery wall around them. The urge to paint graves became so strong that soon the graves spread outside the wall and filled the hillsides (see painting 23).

Next session Michael arrived early for the first time, eager to start. He painted graves and tombstones for the whole session as well as for the following two weeks; his interest never wavered.

Then, one week Michael painted a single grave with a brown cross in the middle of his paper. He also painted a pink body buried under the ground, and he wrote his name in big letters on the wood of the cross (see painting 24). That moment was the culmination of his amazing exploration into life and death. Using his creative freedom to its fullest, he had gone to the end of his creative journey: exploring deep in himself the death of his own body.

This is when Michael painted an apple tree loaded with bright red fruit beside his grave. He ran across the room. "Michele! These are apples; you know I love applesauce! My mom makes it for me!" he said with a tender voice. For the first time he had shared with me about his painting and his life.

Some parents want to stay in touch with their child's process and come to look at the series of paintings done during the terms. I use that opportunity to talk about process and learn about the child's family. Michael's father was truly shocked and worried. "Nobody is sick or dying in our family!" he exclaimed, perplexed.

It took a lot of work to reassure him that it was not an omen but a beautiful expression of Michael's exploration of life through creation. Michael had spontaneously explored his sense of mortality. He had been on a unique quest and had found a way to grow up.

Creators are mountain climbers. They climb the mountain of their inner world, the Dream Mountain; no matter the effort, the climb is joy for the soul. Parents and teachers watching children paint are reminded of the mystery of their own lives. They can only watch and wonder.

When Billy Dared to Paint Blood

*No bird soars too high, if he soars with
his own wings.*

—WILLIAM BLAKE

Children at times need to use raw and intense images;
they need to explore scary subjects as well as mysterious
or fun ones. If adults are not there to stop them, children will dive deep into daring and exciting experiences.

Parents and teachers sometimes can't help but identify with these scary subjects and draw anxious conclusions. I recommend they try spontaneous creative expression for themselves and discover firsthand the great sense of release and even joy in letting dark images come out spontaneously.

Dark images may express a *release of pressure*, the *birth of something new,* or even the shedding of an inner weight. I can only repeat and insist that it is *safe* to let children use them. When children paint dark images, they are listening to intuition and its benevolent and harmonizing force. Children are always safe with it. Please, watch children and observe what happens after they paint these so-called dark images; see how they become joyful and relaxed. Remember that pure and spontaneous expression, no matter the images painted, always brings about the natural healing and integration of feelings.

When children sense that there are no boundaries to what they can do, their passion to create bursts open with enthusiasm. That state of open creativity is infectious and can spread like wildfire in a painting studio.

Billy, a stocky, red-haired seven-year-old, had just painted himself standing, hands at his sides. When he finished painting his body, he painted a small drop of blood dripping from his right hand. With a guilty look he turned his head toward me, clearly worried, waiting for my reaction. I could sense his heavy gaze on me, studying me, wondering if I would indeed punish or stop him. Had he crossed a line?

When he realized that nothing bad was going to happen, he carefully added one more drop. He looked at me, again still somewhat worried. But again my face didn't show any foreboding. I wanted him to feel that nothing wrong was going on and that he was fully free to respond to his creative instinct. He refilled his brush with red paint and dared to paint one more drop of blood and . . . again . . . one more . . . and . . . more . . . Soon, not bothering to check with me anymore, he kept going until the drops blended into one another and covered the bottom third of his painting. The boy in the painting was actually up to his knees in blood. And now Billy wouldn't stop.

"Michele, Michele!" another boy screamed, running at me, alarmed. "Billy is painting BLOOD! Did you see it?"

"So what?" I answered casually.

The other boy, stunned, his mouth half open, looked at me in disbelief. Puzzled, he thought for a moment, then rushed to get some red paint for himself and started to paint blood on his painting.

He put red everywhere: coming out of a truck, mountains, and people. He was glowing with excitement.

Within half an hour all the children were painting blood with abandon, breaking in unison this mysterious taboo. Billy by now had covered his whole background with blood. I kept praying that no one from the school would step into the studio and make negative comments or try to stop us.

Why was it so fascinating for the children to paint blood? They must have thought that if that were permissible, then there were no more limits, no more taboos to their expression. They were feeling the wind of freedom entering the studio and their creations.

Children need to know that their feelings and perceptions are acceptable and that their spontaneous expressions are natural and healthy. They must get the message that there is never a need for shame or repression.

At the end of the session Billy came to me. "My parents are divorcing," he stated, with a deeply concerned voice rising directly from a sorrowful heart. For the first time he was confiding in me as if suddenly he could trust and value my listening. And I truly listened.

When children dive into their creative passions they often spontaneously share secrets or concerns. Trust must be present for it to happen. Usually what they confide is not directly connected with the painting. When this magical moment happens I pay great attention to every word. If they don't volunteer to tell, I fully respect their silence and never intrude by asking questions. My relationship with children in creation is based on respect and on giving them the room to discover on their own who they are and what they need. I always try to create for them a space without influence or pressure.

When children paint, they do not welcome anyone questioning them or forbidding their spontaneous images. I strongly recommend that parents and teachers avoid doing so. If we watch children carefully, we can easily notice how they are hurt by these demands. In trying to explain and justify their images they lose the precious sense of mystery and the indescribable contact with themselves that had developed during creation. They have to leave the truly intimate and personal place of intuition. The sacred experience of creation is then brought back to a mundane level that narrows their creativity and their world.

Exploring Transparencies

Knock on your inner door. No other.

—RUMI

In creative freedom children explore within and without, and at times they experience the delightful adventure of painting transparencies. To paint transparencies is similar to having see-through vision and exploring what is seen under layers of matter. Very simple examples could be fishes in water (see painting 25) or seeing inside a house through the walls (see the illustration on the next page). With transparency children can also express deep feelings by entering aspects of their world that are hidden or impossible to see with the naked eye.

Carole, a vivacious and playful seven-year-old with short curly hair, was deeply absorbed in her creation. She had made an egg with a little yellow chick inside. I was delighted that she had let herself paint *inside* the egg. Her freedom had led her to explore the hidden mystery of her world. She was now painting her house, and again *through* the walls I could see her mother; her little brother was playing with red cars. Suddenly, with tender vulnerability Carole painted a tiny pink baby inside her mother's womb. When she finished she turned to me with a pensive and naked face and said, "I am going to have a baby sister soon."

Carole had not been shown how to paint; she had been given freedom to explore and with it the permission to paint through things and to enter inside them. She was traveling beyond the laws of density and gravity all the way to her heart. Her feelings could unfold in any direction, in any way possible.

Children love to let their intuition and desire for adventure wander inside objects like trees, castles, clouds, animals, and people. Each image can have something inside, which can have something inside; the potential is infinite and quite thrilling. What is painted often can't be seen in the material world. Yet it is created from the demands of powerful feelings and from a need to explore them.

Gravity and opacity are forgotten for the sake of expression

111

and inner truth. Carole originated a world of her own. Her brush explored in and out—no boundaries, no limits, no *should,* no *have to.* Anything was possible. The freedom of not having to follow a model or to make sense was exciting. Adults are often afraid or very tentative about following such spontaneous creative urges for themselves, and they might inadvertently judge the child for it. But they should realize the utmost importance of freedom of expression and never draw a line dividing what is acceptable from what is not. Each piece of creation, when done spontaneously, must be seen as natural, harmonious, and *perfect.* In it, traditional art with its limitation has no place.

In freedom children's posture changes, their whole being becomes involved in what they do and their vibrancy perks up. With full permission to manipulate reality, these young, wild creators become explorers; everything yields to their inventiveness. The shapes, forms, and colors of creativity always surrender willingly and happily to the powerful brush of a free child.

The Coloring Book Trap

Don't give crutches to a child who can fly.

—MC

Parents and teachers need to keep the creative spirit alive in young children. Giving them coloring books equals inadvertently telling them: "Don't explore! Stay within the lines. Don't think of inventing anything, and don't even choose the colors. You are not good enough or old enough to do it on your own; copy what grownups have done." The children, attracted by the brightly colored images, are willing to spend time on them, mechanically filling up the spaces, following instructions. They might be attracted to coloring books because, unlike other books, they can draw in them. They like the fact that parents are interested in them and can show them how to color. They always find pleasure in *pleasing* their parents and also think that parents know best. The activity itself is very automatic, and they only put up with it.

Asking children to work in coloring books gives them a clear and strong message not to use their intuition and their spontaneity, a message that kills their instinct to explore. That indirect communication is bound to weaken or destroy their original power of invention. I think coloring books should be avoided to safeguard children's creative process. Using these books creates the bad habit of relying on someone else's direction for drawing and painting. They become dependent on others' ideas to paint and repress their own creative power.

I was visiting a friend last summer when her three-year-old daughter, Sophia, a vivacious and outspoken little girl, asked me to play with her. I followed her to her playroom. She pulled two coloring books and a few coloring pens out of an open closet. We sat down at a little table, and she opened her book to the next page to be colored and gave me the other one.

"I don't like coloring inside already done pictures!" I exclaimed with playful distaste.

She looked at me intensely and answered with an authoritative voice that wouldn't tolerate any arguing: "I like it. I like it!"

"I don't like to be told what to color and which color to use!" I insisted. She ignored me and began coloring. I started too, but *outside the lines*. I drew a few flowers in the white corner spaces, and some of my colors were intruding on printed images.

Puzzled, she watched me intently, but she didn't utter a word and went on coloring her miserable premade yellow rabbit.

A few minutes later, all of a sudden she started scribbling all over the rabbit. "I don't like it!" she exclaimed with a cunning smile.

Good, I thought. She is coming back to herself.

"Maybe we could find some white paper," I proposed. "I like white paper." She instantly agreed.

We looked everywhere in the filled-up closet among dozens of coloring books. It took us ten minutes to find a little piece of clean paper, even though it had lines on it.

"I like it when there is nothing on the paper!" I said. "I can do anything, absolutely anything I want and you can too. Do you want to invent something?" I offered.

Without answering me she picked a bright red pen and drew with unusual concentration something that could have been a fish. Then her face burst into the widest smile. I winked at her. From then on we were partners.

Keeping Freedom and the Creative Spirit Alive

This chapter contains recommendations that guide parents and teachers to orient and stimulate children's creativity. It expands on how:

- **F**reedom to create propels inspiration and self-reliance
- **L**ifting rules and expectations liberates children's creative power
- **C**riticism, grades, and contests can seriously hinder children's creative power
- **P**arents and teachers can have a major role in their children's creative evolution

Examples of *appropriate responses and comments are given.*

Freedom and the Creative Process

We either make ourselves miserable, or we
make ourselves strong. The amount of
work is the same. . . .

—CARLOS CASTANEDA

Children are very quick to do what adults do: judge their work. The play of their creation is taken away by fear of what the result may look like. Freedom to create can be lost in *an instant* of self-criticism. Then struggle starts. As parents and teachers, we need to teach children *to trust and respect* their work. We need to teach them to look at creativity as *process*.

As adults we are conditioned to judge art expressions; we instantly like or dislike paintings; we quickly decide which part of a work is good or bad and what should be changed or fixed. As a society we are addicted to evaluating the results of our creative work. That attitude paralyzes our intuition. Children feel our judgments toward their work even when we try to hide them. They are *never* fooled. If we want to help children free their creative spirit, we need to reeducate ourselves. We need to break old judgmental habits and learn to look at creativity as process. Then, and only then, can we support children on their creative journeys.

When free from their own judgment, children build creative muscles; their new strength allows them to explore the immense world of creativity *without losing themselves*. Their power of invention grows and their passion blooms. They become *self-reliant*.

From the corner of my eye I suddenly noticed that Jack, a thin ten-year-old boy, was painting over his bright red fire truck. I ran over to him.

"What is happening?" I asked, alarmed.

"It looked stupid!" he said, frustrated. "My water hose looks like a snake!"

"Jack, I wonder how you are looking at that hose. I don't see any problem. Can you let it be? It does not need your opinion. Water hoses sometimes look like snakes, why not? It is intriguing and full of mystery like in a dream or a suspense movie!" I said playfully.

Jack looked at me, first annoyed, then thoughtful. Maybe he *didn't* have to feel bad about what he had done or struggled with. How interesting! There was another way to look at his hose.

"Why don't you *paint back* what you just covered, your strange hose-snake?" I suggested.

To paint back what has just been destroyed is a way to show *respect* to the work and to tell judgment that it is not welcome. It frees the child from a sense of failure and brings back the self-confidence and playfulness that had disappeared with evaluation.

"Okay!" he said, attempting to respond to his painting in a different and more compassionate way. Jack became suddenly so freed by this unexpected approach that as soon as he painted back

Keeping
Freedom
and the
Creative
Spirit
Alive

what he had destroyed, two snakes came to join his hose and coiled around it! He was smiling with intense satisfaction when he put the last touch on the green reptiles' waving red tongues.

"Michele! Can I start over? I did it all wrong!" cried frustrated eight-year-old Kathy, showing me the tender start of a painting. A woman was painted in pink. "What happened?" I asked. "The hands are too big!" she answered, quite upset.

"Oh! No! Oh no, Kathy! It's not wrong; it just came out looking different from what you expected. You were doing well." I put my hand with fingers outstretched very close to her face. "How big does my hand look now?" I asked her.

"Looks big!" she answered.

"Hands have different sizes depending on how you look at them, sometimes they appear bigger than life, sometimes smaller. Interesting, isn't it? There is no problem with your painting. I absolutely *don't* think you have a wrong start."

"Really?" she said, puzzled.

"Yes, really!" I answered with conviction, and *I meant it*.

She reluctantly went back to work. Within ten minutes she seemed to have forgotten about the hands that now were gracefully holding two large yellow daisies. The hands had been painted pink and the fingers carefully traced. Bright red roses were growing around the woman, her mother, standing in a green dress. The obstacle had been conquered. Kathy had found a way to allow her image to be spontaneous. She didn't let herself destroy or manipulate it. She had relaxed and now was enjoying the ease of a non-judgmental attitude. There was no trace of failure in her. It was as it should be.

"Oh! My God! This beautiful purple flower is being smashed!" I said, my hand on my heart. "It hurts!" And it was true: it *did* hurt. Watching a six-year-old child second-guess herself is a very painful sight.

Camille looked at me in disbelief. "It was not good!" she explained pitifully, while covering her blue flower with dark brown paint.

"Oh! I don't think so!" I said.

"It was . . . bad!" she insisted righteously, a tense and sad expression on her face.

"Let's bring back that flower. It belongs here," I said, matter-of-factly. "I'm sure you don't really want to kill that flower. It was growing right here on your painting like in a garden. It's a unique flower like no others. This is what makes it precious. All flowers are different and this one is your special one. You could love it. Next time before you erase anything, remember to call me first. I will show you some magic ways to not judge your work." I winked at her and left her to her thoughts.

In my teaching I work hard at undoing the right-and-wrong judgments. I constantly try to pull out the roots of a conditioning that makes children look at everything they do as success or failure and that makes them grade their work.

Camille needed to understand that there was another way of looking at her work. In the next hour she regained her freedom and with it the unworried joy of painting without self-criticizing.

Parents and teachers should not hesitate to remind children again and again that they are in process when they create, that judging their work does not work and should not be done, that the outcome is not important, that only the doing matters. Children can then discover there is a nonjudgmental way of looking at their painting, a way with freedom.

The Thunder of Criticism

It takes a long time to become young.

—PABLO PICASSO

What moves us the most about children is their vulnerability. Their innocence helps us open our hearts and listen. When children create naturally, they are wide open, in complete surrender of the heart, responding spontaneously to inner urges and longings. They are absorbed in their creation, with mind, heart, and soul moving in unison, roaming in their dreamworld. If someone makes comments or asks questions about their work, thunder roars and jolts them out of that wonderful state. Even if the comment is good, lightning strikes in their creative space. They are pulled out of it harshly and are pushed into the narrow-minded world of success and failure.

In one instant a comment can damage or destroy their carefree spirit because the startled children are asked to enter another reality in which they have to answer for what they do, explain it, correct it, make sense out of it, or be proud or ashamed of it. It is sometimes very hard to understand that a positive comment can hinder creativity. The principle is simple: *Anything that pulls children out of the creative place, out of Point Zero, is not good.* A good comment makes them look at the work as *goods, not as process.* As adults we have been conditioned to believe that compliments stimulate self-confidence and bring support. They do, at times, in some areas in

Flowers don't fly!

Keeping
Freedom
and the
Creative
Spirit
Alive

life. But it is a fact that self-confidence will grow most when children are appreciated for *who they are, not for what they do.* Can our
appreciation be shifted from product to process, from paintings to
painters? Can our appreciation be based on understanding and
respect?

Creativity cannot have two masters. Process and product
don't go together. Children can't create from Point Zero and leave
a part of themselves in the competitive world. It is for us to make
sure that that *split* does not happen.

The Heartless Refrigerator

The main damage would be receiving the message that creativity can be used to get things rather than for the delights of the senses and soul.

—M C

Parents and teachers should not treat children's creative work casually. They need to protect children from the pitiless pressures of the world with its ongoing criticisms and addiction to evaluation by *protecting* their paintings. If we want our children to find lasting creative passion, we should offer them not only a safe place to paint but also a safe place for their work. Children need support in every aspect of their creativity. They need adults to understand the depth and vulnerability of their creative journeys.

Jennifer, a sensitive five-year-old, a gentle soul, heard her older brother say mockingly, "Your cat looks like a big ladybug!"

Feeling powerless, she looked away, a sad expression on her face. She didn't answer him, but something in her shut down, and she aimed a dirty look at the refrigerator.

Jennifer's artwork had ended up on that busy door in the

Keeping
Freedom
and the
Creative
Spirit
Alive

kitchen, vulnerable to grease stains, water splashes, and messy fingers. But that was not all; her precious work was now exposed to comments from anyone who walked into that room, including strangers like her brother's friends or the handyman.

Jennifer had loved painting the cat and the newborn kitties she had seen at her next-door neighbor's. She had poured her heart into making them. Now her poor cat painting was hanging pitilessly on the refrigerator, exposed to God-knows-what and open to criticism.

I am not advocating framing Jennifer's painting and putting it in the living room. The opposite message would be given; the impact would be more compassionate and sophisticated, but in the long run it would be creating the same damage to her newly born creativity.

To single out one painting and expose it to be seen and judged by anyone carries a lot of risks and may simply shut down a child's creativity. The child wonders why that painting was chosen: was it better than others? If Jennifer had received a good comment she would have been pleased and flattered, but she would have felt the pressure to keep up with her success by showing more of her work. She would have struggled to do the next painting beautifully; afraid to fail, she might have decided to repeat what she had done again and again. In other words, Jennifer would have manipulated and used her creativity to produce work that people like. Unused, her intuition would recede and a vicious cycle would start. The act of painting, now a commodity, would become work.

Each of us remembers times where we were not appreciated and how it hurt us. We often think that by going to the opposite extreme we are serving the child's needs. It does not work that way. *True support comes only from understanding.* Could displaying the work be as damaging as criticizing it? Yes! In either case Jennifer would lose her innocent spontaneity and become self-conscious and self-critical. Very likely her intuitive power would diminish or even shut down, depending on her sensitivity and the extent of her reaction to that kind of exposure. Will Jennifer feel again the pure joy and freedom of her creativity and that precious intimacy with her painting? We can only hope and wonder.

I recommend carefully storing children's creative work in art folders. Put a date on the back of each piece and store it with the previous ones. The child, knowing what is done with the paintings, feels an atmosphere of respect for the work. From then on no need to worry; a safe space is created.

Is the Table Standing Straight?

The stem of a flower moves when the

air moves.

—RUMI

Adults often believe that children need to learn the rules of *perspective,* even if later they might have to break them to find their originality. It sounds like a good theory, but unfortunately it does not work that way. When children learn to follow rules in painting, they *lose* their creative integrity. Instead of looking for Point Zero, they think, plan, and apply a technique while looking for expected results. Their intuition and sponta-neous expression, unused, hide in the background. Their creative process loses its potential to have a *natural evolution* of images where perspective is discovered naturally in time.

Andy, an endearing six-year-old with golden curls, had painted with great concentration a brown wooden table and a chair. In her painting she had set the dinner table with plates, glasses, and candles and dressed the chairs with red flowered pillows (see painting 14).

"Now, I am going to paint lasagna," she announced softly to herself. "The grape juice! And oh! The napkins."

She was joyfully adding details when suddenly she painted

a boy rushing into the dining room from the side door. He was pursuing a cat, and the cat was chasing a litter of mice. Andy was playing, immersed in spontaneous inspiration.

When the class was over, her father, who had come to pick her up, glanced through the door and stared at her painting, a puzzled expression on his face. A moment later he asked me, "Why don't you teach her perspective? Her table legs are really off." He had inquired in a cordial tone, but he was genuinely disturbed by my lack of technical instruction for something that seemed so basic to him.

My heart sank because I saw that Andy heard him. The joy on her face suddenly withdrew. She gave me a drowning smile; then, before I could say something, she quickly grasped her father's hand and pulled him out the door, leaving a trail of sadness behind her.

Andy's father had meant well. I realized I urgently needed to start a class for parents, and I was going to begin with a much-needed phone call.

What would have happened if Andy had been asked to straighten her table legs? She didn't know they didn't look like what an adult would expect. They were perfect to her, exactly the way a child her age would want them to be. It was not her lack of technique that was in the way, it was simply that *her perceptions* about space were still *evolving* and at that moment in time needed that stage of representation; they would certainly keep evolving naturally in the future. Left to itself, children's creativity follows an organic evolution. That natural movement has intelligence and must be respected. (See in chapter one, "How the Creative Process Works.")

If Andy had been made to paint her images with standard perspective, she would have had to repress her own way of depict-

Keeping
Freedom
and the
Creative
Spirit
Alive

ing and exploring what she perceived. She would have conformed to a model and would have lost her free and unique inspiration. Painting would have become a task to accomplish, a joyless activity. This is what has happened to most of us during childhood. Let's not perpetuate it.

Can we, parents and teachers, now break the cycle of conditioning through understanding and respect for children's creative spirit?

Can we offer them the deep security that is needed to wander into the extraordinary state of pure inspiration?

Feedback to Give Children

My obligation is this: To be transparent.

—PABLO NERUDA

It is a fact that parents, teachers, and counselors try to support children's creativity, but often they do not know how. Through casual feedback or well-intentioned but ill-advised statements, they may inadvertently undermine children's creative spirit. Children are hungry for true appreciation. They do not want flattery, opinions, or even blind support for what they do. *They want to be seen.* Positive or negative evaluation brings creativity to a superficial level. Parents and teachers should *never compare children's work.* In a studio, nobody is more talented than anybody else.

All children create from who they are in the best way they can. Beauty is in the innocence and truthfulness of their gesture, not in critical aesthetic evaluation. If parents and teachers don't introduce the idea of better and worse, the children won't, either. When children are a little older, they have already been conditioned to think in this way. It is then up to adults to break that unfortunate conditioning. Adults need only to steadily show the attitude of *no competition, no comparison;* children pick it up relatively fast and relax in it.

. . .

"Anytime I show my mother what I have painted or drawn she exclaims, 'It's sooooo beautiful! Sooooo wonderful!'" says Annie, a spirited eight-year-old, mimicking her mother's voice while throwing her arms up. "It does not matter what I show her; she always says the same thing!" And to make her point she added, "Once when I showed her a scribble I had done in a few seconds she said the same thing!"

"My mother too!" echoes her friend Melissa. They both giggled, a touch of sadness in their laugh, dramatizing their moms with their dubious appreciation. "She even says I paint much better than my brother!"

I had overheard the two girls in the corridor during a painting break. Since the beginning of class, the girls had been surprised and a little disappointed not to hear me make any comments, good or bad, about their paintings, but by now they were quite at ease with it. My adult students, parents themselves, often ask me: "What should I tell my children when they show me their paintings if it is not good to comment on them? I truly want to support their creativity."

"Words are tricky," I tell them. "The best way may be to avoid them. Work on changing your attitude; children will respond to a change of attitude. Can you look at creativity as process? Can you see children moving through their creative journeys instead of focusing on the outcome of their work? Can you avoid comparing children?"

To Find out ask yourself these questions:

- Do I really see what children are going through
  when they create, or only the appearance of it?
- Am I aware how they give their heart to creation?

Keeping
Freedom
and the
Creative
Spirit
Alive

- Am I sensitive to how they listen to the mystery of their intuition, to their creative dreamworld?
- Do I see their courage and beauty in daring to express what they do, in fully exploring?
- Can I not compare children's work but instead appreciate all of them for who they are?
- Can I support their process and their experience rather than evaluate the final product with good or bad thoughts or comments?

Often words are not necessary; when they are, very few words are needed; they should concern only the process of creation. Talk about what children already know about their painting process, and show your appreciation or enthusiasm about it. For instance:

- "I can see you enjoyed yourself painting that painting!"
- "It was quite an adventure! Wasn't it?"
- "Aren't you surprised to have painted that painting?"
- "It was fun, wasn't it?"

Children know that creation is mysterious and do not welcome being questioned about what they do. They love their freedom. They paint or create what they *cannot* say, what is beyond words and stories. In my classes, *eye contact* with children has been the most important part of my role as facilitator. I always make sure that they know I see them in their work and that I am *aware* of the movement of their feelings when they paint. There is no need to say anything; our eyes meet, and it is enough. The resulting painting is secondary.

I want the children to discover in their hearts that process is most important. Children want real contact and support in their creative adventures. If they are conditioned to hearing comments, however, they are going to ask for them. If that's all they can get, they will demand them. This is why the belief that the product is what counts must be broken and replaced by real appreciation of creation. If you truly see and understand their process, your eyes will say, "I am with you on your creative journey, no matter what happens, no matter what you paint or go through. *I am with you, here, present.*" If eye contact is not enough to communicate your support, verbalize it. Follow your intuition. If you come from the right place, it will be well received.

Annie's mother had good, loving intentions, but she didn't know how to give support and encouragement, and her intentions backfired. Annie couldn't take her comments seriously. Her mother wouldn't see her creative process; the result—the product—was acknowledged but not the living process. She didn't offer deep attention to her child's work, didn't see the beauty of the act of creation; she saw only colors, shapes, and images on a sheet of paper.

The Damaging Side Effects
of the Art Contest

The trap about success is that you start

imitating yourself.

—UNKNOWN

The temptation of working for product is huge in this world, and children are vulnerable to its promises. Parents and teachers often stimulate children's desires for success by suggesting they participate in contests. I feel it is not a good thing for a child; I recommend that adults avoid doing it. Painting for contests makes children paint solely to succeed—quite a take-off from the free space of spontaneous art. Why put our children through such a stressful experience? Whatever the result, children can't win, because even if they do their creativity will get hurt.

Children need to learn many skills while growing up, but the creative process should be looked at very differently. The goal is not about developing or mastering a skill; it is about children being *completely* on their own and vulnerable in their response. They learn to know themselves, to discover their inner resources, and to act from the whole person. It is not about being rewarded but about allowing authenticity. This makes creativity a very potent, precious, and necessary activity in children's lives. Bringing self-confidence, creativity helps integrate the myriad other activities and feelings that fill children's lives. As guardians of the sacred space of creation, we must offer children a creative space where the pressure to perform is *nonexistent*.

Lydia, a healthy-looking nine-year-old girl, was a gifted student. Her family saw her as an artist-to-be because of her aesthetic sensitivity and her desire to create. When she joined the class she had precise ideas of what she wanted to create and struggled a lot with textures and color blends. The way her paintings looked had become so important to her that it had barred the way to her spontaneous expression. Despite her strong attraction to the arts, she had not met her creative passion.

It took a couple of months for Lydia to find her freedom to create and truly play. Then, endlessly and with great concentration, she painted life scenes and people in the most touching fashion. She loved the class, and she used every minute of it, lost in her paintings. I delighted in watching her paint.

One day, coming back to the studio after an Easter break, she surprised me by tediously painting a red rose in the middle of her blank paper. She reworked it for a long time, trying to make it as beautiful and realistic as she could. After an hour she became tired and disappointed with herself, and she felt so annoyed that just to be finished she carelessly painted a zigzag in the background. The next week she struggled again while she tried to reproduce Japanese bamboo. She fought with green paint, trying to find the best tones and combinations of colors and perfecting her design over and over.

A Lydia I didn't know was painting. Her joy had disappeared and with it her spontaneous, lively images. The inspired child was now under pressure to perform. But why? . . . Why? I wondered.

Later that day I talked with Lydia's mother and found out that during Easter break Lydia had entered and won an art contest. Her behavior suddenly made total sense to me. *Lydia had lost her freedom to create by becoming vulnerable to people's approval.* She was attempting to keep up with her success by making paintings others would like, paintings that could win contests.

It took another month for Lydia to reconnect with her creative passion in our sheltered studio. Will her growing mind remember what had just happened when faced again with the pressure to perform, a pressure that is certain to come her way in the years ahead?

I hoped the seed had been planted deeply enough this time. My work as a teacher was to make sure that seed would become strong enough to withstand the storms to come.

Good and Bad Colors

We only do well the things we like doing.

—COLETTE

There are lots of theories about the best way to help children create. Different techniques and special instructions are designed to ensure good results. This type of instruction does work for many practical skills children need to develop while growing up. They feel empowered anytime they can master a new one. This is very important to their evolution. Children will remember joyfully the first time they were able to do something, like riding a bicycle without help.

Unfortunately, learning a skill is not what creativity is about. Creativity should never be approached as a skill. If it is, what is offered to help children will often hinder the genuine working of creativity. When children have to work within limitations, they lose touch with intuition. Rules and techniques always backfire on children, taking their creative power away. It is hard to imagine the full extent of their damaging impact. The good news is that with the help of an understanding adult, *it takes only a few weeks to a couple of months for children to recover their creative spirit.* When they do, their newfound inspiration gives them a sense of true power.

. . .

Keeping
Freedom
and the
Creative
Spirit
Alive

Amanda, a shy nine-year-old with a tendency to brood, joined the painting class in the middle of the term. She had come from the East Coast and seemed to be having a difficult time adapting to her new life in California.

During the first session she folded into herself and watched with curiosity other children paint. She didn't touch her sheet of paper. At the end of the class, when I was gathering brushes to rinse them, she approached me and in a very timid voice told me, "In my art class at my other school we were not allowed to use *black*."

"Oh! Really?" I answered, surprised. "Why not?"

"It's not a good color, it is a noncolor," she answered matter-of-factly.

"Not for me," I replied. "I like black. I think it's a very intense and powerful color. I do like all colors. I don't think there are good and bad colors; they are just different. Here you can use anything you like and as much as you want. It's like an adventure."

She looked at me, surprised, then doubtful. Finally a cheerful smile burst on her face. "Anything?" she repeated in wonder. "Anything I want . . . ?" And I could sense her wondering if I really meant it.

"Yes! Look at the other children. They invent with all the colors, and at times they use black."

It took Amanda two more weeks to dare to use her colors freely. On that day she painted a deep blue sea on the lower half of her page and an orange half-moon on the top right. She painted a reflection of the moon in the deep waters. Suddenly she covered the sky with black.

With a large black-filled brush still in her hands, she looked at me, shaky and triumphant. She had dared to break an old taboo and reclaim her freedom. She had rescued the bad color and gave it a place of honor in her new California palette.

Why put limitations on children's palettes? Is it that we don't trust them to sense and to know what is appropriate for them? Do we think that if we don't put limits to their creation they would go too far? Can we as parents and adults ask ourselves, "What would it mean for them to go too far?" Reflect for a moment on that question. Are we talking of *our limitations* or theirs?

Creativity, A Natural Urge

Each of us must make our own true way,
and when we do, that way will express the
universal way.

—SUZUKI ROSHI

I
f children are not supported in finding the true source of their creativity, I recommend that they be *left alone* to discover what they can on their own. Children will have a better chance of finding what is essential to them when they are alone than when they are squeezed within boundaries, asked to apply various rules, and expected to perform. Creation is naturally joyful and enticing before constraints are set that prevent children from truly exploring and expressing themselves.

Born into a family of seven children, and being a middle child, I was left to myself. The good side of that situation was that nobody interfered with my creativity. Creativity became the place I would always go when in need of support and strength. It became my steady refuge and sustained me during a long childhood in which I received little emotional nourishment. Whether I used colored pencils or precious and rare paints, whether I made collages or assembled pieces of wood, twigs, stones, and shells, or when I was improvising plays in the hills around my house among the oaks of southern France, my soul explored my feelings and my dreams. Left alone, my imagination would open wild and mysterious expanses and invite me in. I would go there for my daily food, wandering in those vast spaces in which anything was possible.

Watching the new emerge out of me gave my life an anchor and a direction. This secret and intimate place was fully mine, and there I found the strength to survive in a not very friendly world. Creativity rescued me, even though I didn't always know how to carry it further.

Adults were not interested in what I did, so I quickly detached from their possible opinions. I was lucky to have no one trying to influence my creations by praising or criticizing them or even by teaching me techniques.

School was different; there, I became inhibited and afraid of the teacher's judgments, and my desire to belong at times made me compromise. At home, *I had to rely uniquely on myself.* That component was the starting point of my lifelong creative quest. I now realize how lucky I was that I had so little interference with my work. Being fully free, I developed self-reliance and learned to trust my intuition.

The Wisdom of Self-Reliance

*I showed the grown-up my masterpiece,
and I asked them if my drawing scared
them. They answered, "Why be scared
of a hat?" My drawing was not a
picture of a hat. It was a picture of a
boa constrictor digesting an elephant.*

—ANTOINE DE SAINT-EXUPÉRY

Do you know how children sometimes surprise or embarrass us because they say things just the way they are? It is because they still have intact the integrity of their natural perceptions. In a way, this is the true function of self-expression for children: to develop and protect their capacity to respond directly to life, to perceive things as they really are. When children create from a place of freedom, *spontaneous wisdom* develops and helps them not to compromise their needs. They feel what is true for them and trust it.

"Philippe is a very nice student," his schoolteacher told me, a middle-aged, friendly woman. "He is doing well in all subjects, but unfortunately, *he can't paint.*"

Philippe, my son, a quiet and thoughtful six-year-old, was in his first year of academic schooling in Paris, in a public school a couple of blocks from home.

"What . . . ?" I exclaimed, utterly astounded.

"For the last couple of months he has refused to paint," announced the teacher. "I think he is afraid to do it, afraid he can't."

Philippe had been creating since he was a few months old, gripping colored pencils in his unsteady little hand. He had watched me paint since he was born and had always demanded to join me. I remember the time when, at age two, not taking no for an answer he insisted that I give him a very large sheet of paper. I surrendered and pinned an unusually long sheet on the wall of my studio for him. He dipped a big brush in red paint, went to the paper, and painted a thick bright line across it. To go from one side of the sheet to the other side he had to walk a few steps. Intense delight shone on his face as he watched the birth of the long red line that magically appeared out of his paintbrush. It was the most endearing sight to watch him create on a paper so much bigger than himself. I was fascinated to witness that tiny human's ecstatic creative experience.

When Philippe went to school, he was told what to paint and shown what color to use and how. Something inside him must have told him not to become involved with that kind of painting. Those instructions must have felt too foreign and constricted, and he felt no attraction for it. For a couple of months he systematically refused to do it, and no probing succeeded in making him change his mind. He was too used to his freedom to create. His process of inventing had been very private, and nobody had ever judged or praised him. Somewhere inside he must have known not

to jeopardize the intimate and sacred space of his own creation. He had intuitively protected his freedom.

When a child experiences spontaneous expression, a seed is planted, a seed that will sprout in times to come. Even if the child does not create for months or years, the experience of pure creativity stays there, ready to bloom.

Long-Term Effects of Criticism: A Story

I am so small I can barely be seen.

How can this great love be inside me?

—RUMI

During my teaching career I have often encountered adults whose creativity has been blocked for ten, twenty, or even forty years following an incident in childhood, often at an early age. During an unfortunate event, they were made to feel ashamed of what they had created by being criticized, fully misunderstood, or ignored. Children are very sensitive and open, which makes them quite vulnerable. They can easily doubt their ability if an adult (someone who is supposed to know what is right) tells them they did something poorly or wrong. Such comments generate a sense of failure that often goes with the idea *I can't create* or *I can create but I can't be good at it*. The creative spirit is lost. The comment may lead to *a lifelong* attitude of discouragement and an incapacity to fully explore creativity. Much too often I hear such sad stories from my adult students.

Judith, an older woman, her fine face betraying profound emotion, exclaimed at the end of a group discussion in a New York painting workshop, "I just remembered now! I just remembered for the first

149

time! I was in nursery school; I must have been three years old . . .
I was in a room full of pieces of wood, cardboard, and other
things, and I had just built a little toy table. It was a tremendous
feeling. I felt as if I had done something immense. That table felt
huge; it was so alive and s . . . o . . . in . . . ti . . . ma . . . te . . .
so . . . powerful . . . I was feeling as big as a mountain . . . everything was flowing from me. I was trembling with excitement.

"At the end of the day I went to the school hallway to wait
for my father to pick me up; because he was late I was left all alone.
The janitor came in and I proudly showed him my table. 'Look
what I made!' I said, beaming.

"He gave a dull look at my creation and asked, 'What is that?'

"I was shocked by his question. I wondered what was wrong
with him. Later when I looked for my table at home I found out
my mother had thrown it away. She threw away everything I did!"
she added with immense sadness.

Judith was now crying. "I understand now why for so many
years I always created in secret. The last five years I have painted,
and some close friends have said they love what I do. They have
told me I am talented, but I don't feel it inside. Yes, my paintings
are well painted, and I understand why people like them, but for
me I always feel that I am not *fully* engaged, I feel that something
from inside is not passing through me. My paintings are unex-
pressed, not coming from my heart. I have been afraid all along to
let myself go the whole way," she said, staring into her past, tears
streaming down her cheeks.

Then, suddenly, Judith burst open from the inside: ". . . and
I am *sixty-two! Sixty-two!* I can see why I was blocked now!"
she added.

We looked at each other in silence while I watched the three-
year-old come back to life and to a possible freedom. I had just

witnessed the dramatically long-lasting consequences of what had happened to her so long ago and how it had defined her creativity since then.

A week later Judith e-mailed me: "It was not until the class a week ago that I discovered the taste, the sound, and the feeling of my *original* voice. I have reconnected with my table, built by me and lost, now found inside me. I need to inhabit this wonderful free place and let it become my prime way of working. What a blessing!"

Deepening Understanding of the Creative Process

This chapter shows how parents and teachers can nurture the creative element in children to bring forth depths of creativity. It includes:

- **B**asic rules in guiding children toward Point Zero
- **P**recise suggestions and recommendations on how to work with children in special situations
- **H**ow to avoid reactions and carelessness
- **H**ow basic principles have to be remembered and put to work
- **H**ow to use art materials
- **T**he *spiritual* aspects of the creative process

Guidelines for Optimum Creativity

Eleven Golden Rules

1. Always approach creativity as a *process*-oriented activity.
2. Never ask children to paint realistically.
3. Never tell children what to paint or give models to copy.
4. Never correct children's paintings or ask them to fix their paintings.
5. Never *grade, criticize,* or *praise* children's paintings.
6. Never ask children what their paintings represent or why they painted them.
7. Show care, respect, and interest for everything children create.
8. Observe children's process with *understanding*. They must feel seen.
9. *Never compare* children's work. Never encourage competition.
10. When children ask for help to paint, don't show them "how to." Help them realize they can create anything they want.
11. Appreciate children for *who they are,* not for what they do.

Twenty-One Recommendations

1. Never provide creative assignments for children.
2. Never use judgment words, like *good, bad, beautiful, ugly, success, failure, better, worse,* with them.
3. Treat every painting in the same fashion; no preference of one over another.
4. Don't allow children to destroy their paintings. Explore with them to find out if obliterated parts can be brought back.
5. Guide children to keep going until they are truly *complete* with their paintings.
6. When children are finished, ask if they want to write their names on their paintings in any way, anywhere, and in any color.
7. Never try to prevent or react to dark or violent images. They are part of children's expression.
8. Listen carefully when children spontaneously tell you about their paintings, but don't offer your opinion.
9. Ban all coloring and how-to books.
10. Offer white paper rather than colored paper.
11. Have children use good-quality materials (brushes, paint, and paper).
12. Keep the painting setup simple. Don't offer a wide variety of materials (crayons, chalk, pens, collages, engraving, or others) that will distract children.
13. If you are a teacher, keep paintings in the studio until the end of the term to avoid comments at home. At the end of the term have a meeting with the parents to talk about process.
14. Never hang paintings on walls or refrigerators, or anywhere else in view.

15. Never submit children's paintings to contests.

16. Avoid painting with children, especially if they copy you or compare.

17. Write the date and the child's name on the back of each painting.

18. Store paintings with care in a folder with the child's name on it.

19. Show your care for children by doing little things like tying an apron or a shoe, bringing a step stool, or adding a thumbtack to hold their paper.

20. Ask children not to comment on one another's paintings in order to enhance the safety of the studio; if they make a comment, remind them that a painting is a private world where nobody should intrude.

21. Never recommend a child for therapy because you worry about imagery in the painting. Find other reasons if you think therapy may be needed.

Exceptions: Parents and teachers must keep in mind that at special and rare times there might be exceptions for some recommendations and that their intuition should always guide them. When the basic principles of the creative process are understood, the teaching is done from the heart, not from a rigid set of rules.

Filling the White Space

Every perfect traveler always creates the
country where he travels.

—NIKOS KAZANTZAKIS

Parents and teachers often ask, "What am I supposed to do when children leave white space on their paintings? Should I ask them to fill it? Or is it good to have them leave white space around their images?"

What happens to white space is never random and does not show a lack of ability. Empty spaces in children's paintings are precious *landmark*s. They are points of reference in the evolution of their creative process. When very young children start painting, if not interfered with they will always leave empty spaces. This is fully expected and natural.

If we observe what happens to white spaces, we notice that when painting a scene from life, children often paint a ground—a simple brown line or sometimes little patches of earth or green grass (as explained in chapter 1). The rest of the background is left empty. Later they may paint images in the upper part of the painting: clouds, birds, or sun. Then and only then they may feel an urge to represent the sky, often with only a little blue line or traces of colors.

The painting then has a ground, a sky, and in between a large white expanse. The way the ground and the sky are painted expresses children's way of sensing their world. If at this point they are asked to fill the white spaces with colors, they lose the *natural evolution* of their process. They are barred from entering into the exploration of their own perceptions. The creative process is broken, and natural integration is lost. When not interfered with, children spontaneously express their sense of physical presence in the mysterious world of space and gravity by *slowly* filling more of the white spaces from painting to painting. At a certain point in their evolution, which might take a few months to a couple of years, the white space is *entirely* filled with colors. From that point on children will spontaneously keep filling it in every painting; if they don't, a little support will surely make it happen. If some white space is left, the teacher knows that the child has not gone as far as possible. It's a sign that feelings are moving sluggishly or are blocked and that the child needs to be stimulated and encouraged to go deeper; the child needs support.

Sometimes children do not paint scenes from life, but the process is the same. If children are left free, the white areas will slowly fill. Often they are covered first with lines or dots until one day a solid color expands and fills the whole space. It is crucial for children to *go through the process of conquering space without anyone suggesting or interfering in any way,* lest the process of integration and discovery be lost.

When we stimulate children to do more on a painting that appears incomplete, we should *never* ask anything specifically. It is for them to find spontaneously what is next. Parents and teachers should strongly avoid suggestions and never ask, "What could you paint THERE?" or "Can you extend that color?" That would defeat the purpose of the creative process. On the other hand, the stimulation we can give is oriented toward bringing back children's inspiration and letting them move from there. It is meant to encourage them to dig into themselves, to go deeper in the unknown of their inner world. Our interaction is to help them stretch their creative muscles but never to interfere with their painting process.

Letting Go of Special Effects

Worshipping the teapot instead of drinking the tea.

—WEI WU WEI

As long as children believe adults have a lot to teach them about how to paint, they will remain distant from their intuition. If adults show them clever ways to obtain *special effects*, children can become fascinated for entertainment's sake. Special effects, like how to paint eyes that smile, how to paint a certain perspective, how to do shading, and how to paint three-dimensionally, are often offered to children. There are endless lists of *how-tos*. All these particular tricks or techniques *interfere with* or even stop children's ability to paint from intuition, to invent from Point Zero. I recommend that parents and teachers never encourage children to paint in *a mechanical* way for a particular effect or to reproduce anything according to a set of instructions.

I am not saying that at a certain point children should not get help on how to mix or use paints or brushes to get better control over them, but that this should happen only *if and when* they need it in the development of their process. Children will generally ask for help with a precise image, for instance, asking for a special color for a sunset. Then I will have them describe the color to me, and I will have them explore how to make it themselves through trial

I love my painting!

and error. When they ask me how to paint something, I lead them to find the answer *within* themselves. I give direct information only when it's very practical and absolutely necessary.

As a basic rule, children should never be told how to paint. The area of creativity should be a virgin land for them, a place of their own where no intruder can get in. If they are offered a technique or a trick, they will use it, believing it is going to help, thereby forgetting the beauty and endless inspiration of their intuition. Not only may they lose touch with their inspiration, but also they may become accustomed to coming from their heads instead of their hearts. When offered these techniques, children learn to plan and compromise and often end up working solely to see their effects. The *purity* of their expression may then be lost.

This is why teaching special effects to children may lead to a dead end. Children inevitably tire of special effects and can be left uninspired and discouraged. The more damaging and sad outcome is that from then on, children will look for stimulation from the outside instead of looking inward for their inspiration.

Splashes, Drips, Scribbles

It is good to have an end to journey toward;

but it is the journey that matters in the end.

—URSULA K. LEGUIN

For children an easy way to avoid their feelings is to splash, scribble, or drip paint on top of what is already painted. They may think it is fun for a while, but it soon leaves them tired and uninterested. As adults it is our role to interact with children during those times and bring them back to process.

SPLASHES

"Ah! Ah!!" said an excited John, using a large brush and throwing yellow-green paint from a distance onto his painting. He had just finished painting a bridge with a couple of fluorescent orange canoes crossing underneath. Yellow-green splashes were landing everywhere.

"John! You can't throw paint on your painting like that! You are destroying it, and your neighbor is getting splashed too!" Amie, who had been painting by his side, was getting quite upset. Four or five little splashes had landed on her careful mountain scene.

"I need to do that!" John replied stubbornly. "A big storm is coming in!"

"Could you find another way to paint your storm? Could you find something you can paint with your brush instead of letting it happen at random?"

John, still excited by the catharsis of throwing paint, didn't listen to me.

"John! Do I need to call you on the phone for you to listen to what I just said? Think for a while. How else could you paint the storm if you didn't splash? Tell me, how big is your storm?"

John looked at me. "Real big!" he exclaimed proudly. "Maybe I could paint a big wave coming from the side . . . It might even overturn one of the boats," he added, taken by this sudden idea.

Within a few minutes and with great excitement, John painted a monster wave. Then lightning hit the bridge, and the wind threw everything into the air. There was no more need for splashes.

DRIPS

"Janine, your blue paint is dripping all over!" I exclaimed, concerned. The watery paint was coming out of freshly painted clouds. "You could have called me! I could help you stop the drip with my painting knife."

"I want to keep them," she answered "It's rain; it's raining."

"Having rain on your painting, why not? But why don't you paint it directly instead of by accident? Do you know why your color is dripping?"

She hesitated; she thought for a moment and moved her head sideways. "No, I'm not sure. Did I put too much paint on my brush?"

"What do you think made your color drip? Let's go and check it out." We went together to the paint table, and I showed her what the paint did when there was too much water in it.

"Yes, I understand," she said with a mature look.

Janine returned to her painting. She painted blue rain on one side of her painting only; a few minutes later a bright sun suddenly appeared on the other side.

SCRIBBLES

Tiffany was painting a pink woman with a blue dress. I am not sure what happened, but when I was not looking she had scribbled all over it.

"Oh, my God!" I exclaimed. "What is going on?" She lowered her eyes; her face stern and upset. "I did it all wrong; there was not enough room for her feet and arms!"

"Tiffany, it's never good to scribble on top of something. It destroys what you have done, and it hurts. You didn't make a mistake; your image just happened to be big because it wanted to be big like in a dream. It could be fun not to have to paint every part of that woman. If you really need more room we could add a piece of paper underneath, as much paper as you want."

Tiffany suddenly relaxed when she heard she could add more paper. Big feelings were in her and she had needed space, but she had not known how to find it. Scribbling was a reaction to the dead end she had felt caught in.

Starting over is often thought as having a chance for a more interesting start. Children want to do it when they think they have failed. When is it appropriate? When parents and teachers look at what the child does from the point of view of process, they can sense that most of the time the child didn't make a "wrong" start but was expecting a different result. There is no question of failure. *Intuition* made the child paint something "too" big or "too" small or make an unusual shape. It is no accident.

When children are ready to explore the unknown and move

in process, they rarely ask to start again. There is a danger associated with starting over. It creates in the child's mind a critical view of beginnings that introduces concerns about performance. The Point Zero approach teaches children to *respond creatively* to difficult situations instead of reacting to them. Adults should always be very careful and thoughtful before considering a new start for a child's painting.

Expression versus Catharsis

Not knowing when the dawn will come

I open every door.

—EMILY DICKINSON

We want children to express themselves, but we don't want them to react and confuse creation with catharsis. *Catharsis is not creation; it is only a release of pressure.* When children paint in a cathartic way, they paint as if they were beating a pillow. They usually are in a state of tension, painting without respecting what they did before, mistreating the brushes, and making a mess.

Cathartic paintings happen sometimes at the beginning of children's process. They feel so lost about finding their creative inspiration that they paint by using quick and wild scribbling gestures (not to be confused with the natural scribbling that very young children do when they first start painting). Sometimes they even try to dip their hands in the paint and apply them to the paper or use sponges or other props for quick and wild actions. They get rid of nervous energy in that way, but they do not move toward Point Zero. When they finish they feel better for a few minutes but have nothing to go on with.

How can we guide children to tap into their creative potential and find Point Zero when they are so full of nervous energy and impatience? We can do it by bringing them back to themselves beyond their superficial reactions and by interesting them in inventing. We need *to stay by their side* until they find an authentic thread to follow. We can ask them questions to stir their creative potential out of its sleep.

Questioning should always be playful and full of enthusiasm about the possible outcome. We could, for instance, ask with excitement:

- "What would you do if you could paint absolutely anything in the whole world, without worrying? If you could *really* do anything?"
- "What could you paint if you could paint slowly and with care?"
- "What if you could start with one big (or small) image?"
- "What if you could paint something about *your life*?"

These questions encourage children to feel without forcing them into a particular outcome. We offer a general direction, a vast space, but we are focusing on their feelings of the moment.

Natalie, one of my adult students, a thoughtful and spiritual woman, was so taken by her own process that she decided to start teaching children. One day she came to class, a bright smile on her face and with a stackful of children's paintings for me to look at. "The children love to paint!" she exclaimed. "I am so touched watching them express themselves. They love the freedom I give them."

We looked at four weeks of paintings that had been sorted in chronological order. Most had been cathartic. For four weeks their creativity had not really been stimulated. I couldn't detect any evolution toward Point Zero. The children had not found their creative stream and were confusing releasing with creating. Yet they were happy, because compared to the usual restrictions and demands of other classes, they had a lot of permission and fun.

Natalie could have brought them back to their feelings by asking them questions and by asking them to slow down. She could also have taught them how to hold their brushes correctly and how to put the right amount of paint and water on them. (Their paintings showed a misuse of painting materials.) These two recommendations alone might have helped a great deal. Children need to be told how to use tools in the best way. It creates *order* in the painting gesture, and out of that, creative energy is stimulated.

Natalie also needed to help children complete their paintings. It was her role not to let them finish too quickly. Children can face more of their feelings by going further into what they have already painted. When I challenge children to continue on their scribbled paintings, I often see shy little images appear in corners or in the most unexpected places. These images announce a contact with Point Zero and are the birth of images that will often be spontaneously repeated in the following painting. If children are left to their impatient reactions, they will want to be finished with their paintings faster and faster, never facing the inner need to uncover and explore their dreamworld.

Show your encouragement and appreciation with eye contact anytime a child moves toward Point Zero. No words are needed. The child, *feeling seen,* becomes more and more willing to explore. If we seem happy with catharsis, the child will *continue* doing it. To give real support to children, we need to develop insights into how process works, use our intuition, and never settle for catharsis.

Allowing Strong Images

Who has not sat before his own

heart's curtain?

It lifts: and the scenery is falling apart.

—RAINER MARIA RILKE

I am a very determined, nonviolent person. When Philippe was born I decided I would never give him toys that could stimulate aggressiveness in him. When he was two or three years old, he met children who played with small colorful plastic water pistols. He wanted one. I refused and held steadfast.

One day I found him in the garden shooting at imaginary things. I came closer and discovered a little piece of wood in his hand, a twig in the vague form of a gun. I realized that I had been unrealistically stubborn and bought him the yellow water pistol he had wanted for so long. The toy gun helped him work out and express the intensity of his feelings.

Being a little person in this grownup world full of mysteries can be quite stressful at times, and Philippe had a lot to express and to explore. I shouldn't have taken his playful needs literally. That toy, I had to admit, never stimulated anger or violence in him. I am never in favor of war toys that might truly stimulate violence. But that day in the garden I was sorry it had taken me so long to trust my young son's innocent desires.

This experience was God-given for me, because when I started to teach painting I was at ease with children's dream imagery even when they expressed frustration and anger. I gave permission for strong and violent images in their paintings. I didn't worry about them or take them literally, believing there were problems. I saw only release of pressure and need to explore (see paintings 18 through 22) I knew the paintings were portraying the dreamworld, and the dreamworld needs striking images and unfamiliar disguises. I was careful not to create limits for the children or to censure their spontaneous expression. I was there to trust their natural instinct and the *benevolent force* of creativity. I found out that a pure creative process never goes out of line and never brings a threatening situation. As a result, in my studio the children could sense the extraordinary freedom to express and explore anything. They had permission to be themselves. My young painting students grew in strength and confidence as they rode the winding roads of growing up. They became more quiet and happy because the pressures of their lives now had a way to be released and become constructive. Their frustration and anger could turn into spontaneous creations instead of creating havoc and dangerous behavior.

Setting Up a Painting Studio

The mind cannot act the role of the heart.

—FRANÇOIS DE LA ROCHEFOUCAULD

C hildren can paint in many settings. Here are a few ideas to help you set up your studio space. You don't need a perfect setting; depending on your situation, you may need to improvise. The main motto is: *Keep it simple and available to children.*

Painting places or studios can be arranged easily and be quite efficient. If you do not have the best possible place, remember that the principles of creativity and the spirit of the method are what count.

HOME SETTING
FOR ONE OR TWO CHILDREN

Finding a place: A wall works as well as an easel—you can cover it with soft fiberboard for gripping tacks or a piece of cardboard to which you can tape paper. You can also create a painting place by covering a wall with wrapping paper or plastic and using masking tape or thumbtacks to hold paper. I recommend that children paint standing up. It keeps stamina going and allows them to use larger sheets of paper. Get a clip-on lamp to light the paper and a small table or shelf to hold the paints and brushes. Protect the floor with a carpet remnant or a piece of cardboard.

For *palettes,* put paint in ice cube or muffin trays, a different color in each hole. Fill only halfway. I recommend water-based paint like tempera. Offer at least eight colors; the more the better.

When children use the palette, always make sure that colors do not get mixed or dirty. Always keep a clean palette. If a new color is needed, mix it in a new place; metal jar lids work well.

On the paint table set *two jars* (plastic or glass) of water, one for dipping *brushes* with dark paint, one for *brushes* with light paint. Another empty jar could hold different-sized brushes. Always stand the brushes with bristles pointing up. Brushes should never stand on their bristles.

Gather a few brushes of different sizes, including a very small one for details. I recommend pointed brushes. Teardrop-shaped brushes are best.

Use a *spray bottle* to moisten drying paints. Have *tissues* and *rags* available and a *rounded knife* to mix colors. An *apron with a pocket* always helps.

When the painting session is finished, *spray the palette* with water and cover it with plastic; then put it in the *refrigerator* to keep it fresh and ready to use at all times. The paint will keep for months or even a year if it is kept moist.

Instead of tempera, other options include watercolors, markers, crayons, and felt pens. For more details on which materials to use, see the appendix.

STUDIO SETTING
FOR TEACHERS' CLASSES

This is a very efficient setting and one I have often used. The French educator Arno Stern, who has done research on children's creativity and developed his own method of work, invented it a few decades ago. His ideal painting studio consists of a small rectangular room with a long, narrow central painting table. The table has holes to hold two dozen paint colors in jars and a jar of water for each color. (See photo 26.) Each color also has three different-sized brushes. Large sheets of paper, 20 by 24 inches, are pinned to the walls. The painters stand and move back and forth from paper to table to take brushes and colors they need. It is a very efficient system because the brushes never need to be washed; they always hold the same colors and are put back where they belong after each use. Children paint standing up and can have the option of expanding their paintings by adding more paper.

PARENTS' HOME STUDIO SETTING
FOR A GROUP OF CHILDREN

Read the setup for studio classes and see how you can make a studio. Prepare only one paint table that children learn to use communally. A small table could be set up in the middle of the room. Each paint container (round plastic 4-ounce Tupperware-type containers work well) needs a water container to match it; 8-ounce plastic cups work well. Brushes are placed, lying beside the corresponding paint and returned there after each use.

Garages sometimes lend themselves well for this purpose. If not, a corner of a family room or veranda might offer the right space. Use old carpets or carpet remnants for the floor. Make sure the light is bright enough so children don't strain their eyes, and keep the place quiet and private for the duration of the painting session. Remove and store paintings before allowing others into the space, so they won't be able to comment on and criticize the work.

To create a studio atmosphere, don't mix activities. Keep that special time just for painting. Depending on the children's ages, it is best to limit the session to half an hour to an hour to start. The time can later be extended to two hours. An adult should stay with the children at all times for order, structure, support, and inspiration. Each child should have a portfolio where his or her paintings are kept. The child will feel safe, knowing where they are.

How to Use Art Materials

*Order in the studio creates a sense of
security and support.*

—MC

To explore the power of creativity, children need *clear boundaries* and good organization in the studio. A safe context allows them to enter the deep mystery of the unknown. Adults should be aware of how children are painting and help them use art materials in the most *efficient* way. They may have to *repeat* instructions time after time until children have integrated them into their practice.

Children need to understand the simple, commonsense rules on the basis of one principle: *Treat the art materials in a way that will make them perform well and last long.* When children understand what *not* to do, adults' demands won't appear arbitrary but reasonable. For instance . . .

"My red paint turned brown!" exclaimed Annie, disappointed.

"Why do you think it did?" I asked her.

She thought for a while and then realized that the black paint underneath was not dry.

"Annie, you need to look at your painting at an angle. When it shines, it means it's not dry. You must wait. You can bend your head to the side and look. You will see that it always shines when it's not dry."

Children should be taught to respect and care for their painting tools. They need to understand how the brushes work and how precious they are. Contrary to what many people think, to fully bloom in their creativity children need good-quality materials, not cheap ones. They have less control in holding their brushes than adults do. A good-quality brush follows the gesture faithfully and translates the subtleties of the children's efforts. When a brush is held well with the right amount of paint and water on it, children are more likely to be able to paint in a satisfying way. A poor-quality brush does not follow the gesture. It does not go where it is intended, and this can be very discouraging. Children need the best.

Children should learn to keep the painting table clean and efficient by putting back the brushes where they found them and by dipping the brushes only in colors meant for those brushes. If they make a mistake, they should let the adult know immediately and help clean it up.

If a child needs a special mix, do it outside the basic setup. Children can learn how colors blend by putting a tiny amount of paint on a fingertip and a different color on a fingertip on the other hand and then rubbing the two fingers together. They can also do it in a little dish using a paint knife. Children then explore how to make their own colors and put them on their paintings only when they have found what they want. It is much safer and more accurate than mixing colors on paper. In that way they learn the precise amount needed for creating the color they want. I always ask children to make a new color only when they really need it. Otherwise, they could spend the whole session making colors and avoiding facing the creative void.

We help children by showing *how to* for practical matters—for

material painting needs—but only for these needs. As parents and teachers, we never want to enter the private space where their intuition should be used.

This practical attention creates a well-needed structure and impresses on children that adults care. Order in the physical world creates a safe and friendly context that allows the children to soar into their creativity.

I recently asked my two-year-old granddaughter to experiment by holding her brush differently. She reacted to my suggestion by throwing me a dark look and by pushing harder on it. But within a few minutes of hearing my enticing explanations, she became interested in trying. She then held her brush as I suggested: *not pushing too hard* and painting only with the tip, and filling the brush with water *every time* before adding paint. She smiled, astounded at the result. The brush was now painting a full soft line instead of a scratchy mark. Her brush had found power because it could follow her gesture. Moments later I witnessed her painting her first form (she had only scribbled and splashed before), a mysterious, well-formed shape.

Children love to master the use of their tools. Good workmanship enhances and stimulates their power of expression.

The Spiritual Aspect of Creativity

Let the drop of water that is you become a

hundred mighty seas.

—RUMI

To create from the source is to enter spirit. I am not talking about religious beliefs but about the ability to contact the greater dimensions within. Pure creativity brings out the desire to explore the unknown dimensions of our lives and to look upon the larger perspective of the immense universe.

Children, as much as adults, long to use themselves fully and explore the mystery of life. Young children have an acute sense of mystery and an inborn contact with spirit, and when they learn to use their intuition they stay in touch with those qualities. Creativity brings a strength so basic and solid to their lives that it actually changes how they perceive themselves and their world. More space is created, and they develop trust in the life force and in the greater power that created them.

The Point Zero method touches all aspects of children's lives and allows them not only to enter into their feelings but to actually *reestablish contact with the unknown.* It keeps minds and hearts open to face the ongoing riddle of existence and turns the heart toward spirit. On the practical level it stimulates the development of a less judgmental character, one more willing to flow with things and respond to unexpected situations.

The Point Zero method not only pertains to painting; it can be used for any creative endeavor. When the basic principles of creativity have been understood and assimilated, they can be used daily in our interactions with children. They support children in using their intuition, in trusting and expressing themselves in all parts of life. Whether children are writing, dancing, gardening, cooking, or doing music or sports or other creative activities, they will be more apt to find their own voice and their own strength by using the Point Zero method. In any of these activities an adult can ask, "What would you do now if you could follow your feelings, if you could invent spontaneously? If you could trust?" The child is then encouraged to explore from within and to deal with obstacles in creative ways.

Children's behaviors change because their intuition is used spontaneously in everything they do. Their outlook on life evolves, bringing them greater security and enthusiasm. Through creativity, children realize the immense potential that lies within themselves. When with adults' help children become familiar with the source of creativity, they can face growing up by dipping into that infinite and mysterious place. Creativity becomes an invaluable tool they can use for a lifetime, a means to meet the challenges and demands of living from a place of passion, wisdom, and spirit.

Often when adults see the profound effects of creativity in children's lives, they remember their own potential to create. They suddenly feel pulled to paint, to paint in freedom, for process not product. They become aware of their need for self-expression and self-exploration. Inspired by children to enter their creative process, adults follow their children's steps. Creative passion then flows with its spirit in both child and adult worlds.

Art Supplies and Where to Buy Them

The painting process is not tied to certain materials, but for children I like to use easy–to–spread, quick-drying, water-based paint.

Tempera paints lend themselves well to the painting process. They should be of good quality. They are not costly. If you already have other paints, you can try using them. Some children respond to watercolors, but I consider them a second choice. They are not as opaque as tempera, and the use of so much water is often a distraction for children.

COLORS

Children need at least six basic colors to get started: white, red, blue, green, yellow, and black. You can mix these colors to make different ones. If you can purchase six more colors, purchase pale blue, orange, brown, violet, peach, and magenta. (Peach, pale blue, and brown are much needed by children.) For a class I recommend six additional colors: pink, lavender, burnt sienna, gray, ochre, yellow-green, dark red, and dark green.

BRUSHES

I recommend using good brushes that, if well taken care of, can last many years. Make sure you *don't buy brushes meant for acrylic paint.* They are too hard, hold very little paint, won't release it well, and won't work well with tempera paint.

Don't purchase square or flat brushes. *Brushes should be pointed so children can control their lines.* Drop-shaped brushes are best.

Yarka brushes numbers 10, 8, and 6 are of good quality and are moderately priced.

Isabey 6227z–2 watercolor brushes are teardrop-shaped and pointed brushes, known as round brushes, and are expensive. An assortment of three or four brushes is good to have. Most good brushes come in different sizes. Good sizes to start with are numbers 000, 2, and 3.

The Loew-Cornell Standard quality synthetic brushes also work well: numbers 6, 10, and 14, in the 7000 series, round, as well as the 7350–1 liner. These are moderately priced.

You can use any other watercolor brush that will hold enough paint and will follow the gesture. You can buy Utrecht numbers 6 and 12.

PAPER

Art stores carry many qualities of paper. The paper *should not be too grainy or too smooth.* Avoid paper that absorbs too much or not enough paint.

Another option is to buy printing paper. You can buy it in batches of 200, 500, or 1,000 sheets. 80 lb. Vellum Bristol works well, 20 by 26 inches or 22 by 28 inches.

Brands: Springhill, Wasau Exact, and others. You can find printing paper through printing paper suppliers, and it is very cheap. They will cut it into the size you want. Check paper suppliers in your area or on the Internet.

There are a lot of art supply mail-order companies. Two are:

Nasco: 800–558–9595 or 920–563–2446
Sax Arts and Crafts: 800–558–6696

Acknowledgments

I give my heartfelt thanks to Jeremy Tarcher for his unending enthusiasm and care in helping me form and edit this manuscript and for his valuable understanding and trust in my work. I also thank my first editor, Sue Mann, who helped me from the start of this project with her useful and inspiring suggestions, as well as my second editor, Terri Hennessy.

I extend my grateful thanks to the dear friends who supported the birth of this book: Diane Hullet who looked over the manuscript a few times; Barbara Rifkin, Carol Levow, Margrit Haerberlin, Nan Holmes, Bob McIntyre, Lynn Newman, Samantha Borinstein, Graham Best, and Carol McIntyre for their affectionate encouragement and support; and George Rosenfeld for helping me with the illustrations and cover.

I give many thanks to Arno Stern, who, in my early twenties, inspired me to work with children, let me benefit from his discoveries about children's creativity and let me paint in the children's studio, an experience that launched me on my creative adventure. I send my gratitude to my son, Philippe, my two granddaughters, and all the many children who have allowed me to work with them and make this book possible. And most of all I thank the creative process for having brought to my students and to myself joy, passion, and spirit.

About the Author

I was born and raised in southern France in a family of seven children. As a young adult, I moved to Paris, where I studied law, literature, and art. After desperate attempts to fit into the art education system, I had to admit that traditional art schools were not for me. To my distress, in the various art classes I attended I hadn't found ways to explore the true potential of my creativity. I had not found self-expression, nor had I even touched the mystery of creation.

"Michele, painting is not for you," my last art teacher had declared. Sadly, I gave up painting and with it my lifelong dream of dedicating myself to the arts. Because I seemed to be without any talent for painting, I decided to become a facilitator of children's creativity. I had heard of the *Free Expression Studio,* in the heart of Paris, led by Arno Stern, where children could paint without being graded or judged in any way, and I had become very intrigued.

When I first walked into that marvelous art studio to observe the children—fourteen of them, aged five to fifteen—they were already painting. I was so touched by what I saw that I burst into tears. Creativity was moving in the room, real, almost tangible. For so many years I had been wanting to be taught, but at that moment I fully realized that *what I needed was not instruction but freedom and spontaneity*. I saw the immense necessity of trusting my own intuition.

In meeting those children I found a true starting place for my creative quest. I recognized it as what I had been looking for for so many years. It had not been an impossible fantasy but an obvious, solid, real option; at last, my passion had found a place to grow.

Instantly, I wanted to paint in that studio; I wanted to be one of the children, away from the adult world of art with its rules and expectations. I wanted to give myself the permission to fully follow my creative instinct. I also wanted to learn all I could about creativity from this unusual man, researcher, and educator.

Although I was the only adult student, the children accepted me graciously as one of themselves. I painted every day with them for more than three years. I quickly found freedom of expression. My creativity, finally uninhibited, exploded, and I became so passionate that I couldn't stop painting. Creativity touched my whole being: it changed my life inside, in the way I perceived myself, and outside, in how I related to the world. It changed everything; through creativity I had found my inner voice.

From the start a burning desire to share my discoveries made me a teacher, or *unteacher,* as I like to call myself. I first started experimenting in my home with groups of children and adults. Then I taught in a social center in Paris. Later I moved to Canada, where I worked in schools, community centers, and homes for children with special needs. I also worked for a few years with academic students at the University of Ottawa. When I moved to the United States I called my work the Painting Experience and co-ran a studio with that name for twelve years (currently a *different* teaching goes on under that name). My work is called the Point Zero method. Through the years I have been privileged to *unteach* thousands of students, both children and adults, and have watched with delight their launching into the great adventure of creation.

My teaching has evolved from my own painting process and from observing my students. The painting stories in this book took place in studios and schools, both public and private, throughout the years. Whether I am teaching or painting, my enthusiasm has never faltered, *because true creativity gives newness to everything it touches.* To this day I am still discovering new depths to the mysterious and fascinating process that has filled my life.

A passionate artist, Michele has painted over five thousand paintings and makes videos of her work. She is known internationally for her groundbreaking work in exploring the spiritual dimensions of the creative process. She presently teaches the Point Zero method under the name *Michele Cassou Painting Workshops* and lectures in the San Francisco Bay Area and at the Esalen Institute in Big Sur, California, the Open Center for Learning in New York City, the Mabel Dodge Luhan House in Taos, New Mexico, and many other locales in the United States and in Europe. She lives in San Rafael, California.

Contact Information

To receive information on Point Zero Painting Workshops, books (including *Point Zero, Creativity without Limits,* and *Life, Paint and Passion* and two booklets, *The Question Book* and *The Buddhist Art Doctor*), and audio and videotapes (including *Birth of a Process* and *Point Zero, Insights and Images*), please contact:

MICHELE CASSOU PAINTING WORKSHOPS
Tel: (415) 459-4829 or (415) 721-3812
Fax: 415-459-4829
369-B Third Street PM B 279
San Rafael, CA 94901
website: www.michelecassou.com
e-mail: Cassouart@aol.com